WORLD FAMOUS
SPIES

WORLD FAMOUS
SPIES

Damon Wilson

||| ·PARRAGON· |||

This edition published and distributed by Parragon,
produced by Magpie Books,
and imprint of Robinson Publishing, London

Parragon
Unit 13–17,
Avonbridge Trading Estate,
Atlantic Road,
Avonmouth,
Bristol, BS11 9QD

ISBN 0 75251 783 X

British Library Cataloguing-in-Publication Data
A catalogue record for this book is available
from the British Library

10 9 8 7 6 5 4 3 2 1

CONTENTS

Spies

Chapter One

THE TRADE OF TREACHERY

A ll crime is a form of betrayal. But in the 20th century, one form of betrayal, espionage, has been recognised as a political necessity, and given a kind of dubious respectability. The moral dilemma involved has fascinated writers like Graham Greene and John Le Carré, one result being the immense popularity of the spy novel in the second half of the 20th century. If, as seems likely, the downfall of the Soviet Union puts an end to the need for 'cold war' politics, our grandchildren may look back with nostalgia on the 'age of espionage' that came to an end about 1990.

But what about its beginnings?

Alexander The Great

Well, if spying means the gathering of information by betrayal and stealth, then one of the earliest recorded examples concerns Alexander the Great. In 327 BC, Alexander – who had already conquered Greece and Persia – led his army towards India. Many of his men were reluctant to go, and Alexander heard rumours of a plot to assassinate him.

At the next encampment, he announced that he intended to send a heavily guarded cart full of mail back to Greece, and that anyone who wanted to write home should do so now. These, he guaranteed, would arrive unopened. Every-

Field Marshal Montgomery once described the biblical prophet Moses as 'the greatest general of all time.' The Prophet was also, with the help of God, an exemplary spymaster – as this passage from the Book of Numbers shows.

'And the Lord spake unto Moses saying: Send thou men that they may search the land of Canaan . . . And Moses sent them to spy out the land . . . .

'Go up into the mountain . . . and see the land, what is; and the people that dwelleth therein, whether they be strong or weak, few or many.

'And what the land that they dwell in, whether it be good or bad, and what cities that be that they dwell in, whether in tents or strong holds; and what the land is, whether it be fat or lean.

'So they went up and searched the land.'

This is as concise and effective a briefing as any laid down by the CIA or KGB policy departments.

one believed him, and most of his officers wrote letters home.

As soon as the mail cart was out of sight, Alexander followed it, and spent the next few hours opening and reading all the letters. Several of them were written by the would-be assassins and described the plot, and the names of fellow-conspirators. Alexander then returned to camp, and had the plotters arrested and executed. They included his second-in-command Parmenion, whose son was one of the plotters; Alexander knew that he would have to kill the father, or face a blood feud.

Confronted with the problem of whether to admit breaking his word, Alexander decided to tell the truth. Fortunately, his army took the view that it was a brilliant piece of detective work, and admired his cunning. But Alexander himself was so depressed by his skulduggery that he refused to eat for more than a week, and finally had to be force-fed by his friends.

Mithradates the Great

Two centuries after Alexander, the first man – as far as we know – to use spying to achieve military conquest was a Turk who is now known as Mithradates the Great. In fact, Turkey did not then exist – it was confusingly known as Asia – but Mithradates was born in the part that was then called Pontus, on the Black Sea.

His father died when he was young, almost certainly murdered by his mother (whose name has failed to come down to us), a highly ambitious woman who intended to rule via her eleven year old son. But young Mithradates proved to have a mind of his own, and when several unsuccessful attempts had been made on his life, he took the hint, and fled into exile, leaving the throne to his younger, more tractable brother.

His years as a fugitive were not wasted. As he wandered around Asia Minor, he learned twenty-two languages and dialects, but soon realised that this was not enough if he wanted to to go unnoticed. So, like Kipling's Kim, he used to disguise himself as a street urchin, and study the local customs and dialect until he could pass as a native. Nobody paid much attention to the shabby teenage beggar, so he was able to wander wherever he pleased, and study the lie of the land while he learned about the size and disposition of their defensive forces. After several years of information-gathering, he returned to Pontus a wiser and rather more dangerous young man.

He soon organised a coup in which he overthrew his mother and younger brother — he imprisoned them both, and later had them executed. (It has to be admitted that Mithradates was a particularly unpleasant young man, but no more so than most rulers of the time.) And now he put to use the knowledge he had been acquiring for years. He already had in his head a plan for overcoming all the small cities and states around him, and he carried it out with masterly force and economy. As his army marched in, they fell like ninepins, dazed by his apparently supernatural knowledge of their defences.

The remainder of the story of Mithradates illustrates the problems of a man who bases his life on treachery and deceit. When he decided to murder all the Roman citizens in his domains, he became the chief enemy of Rome. All his skill in spying was of no help when a Roman army arrived on his doorstep in 88 BC, and he would certainly have lost his head if the Roman general — Sulla — had not been forced to hurry back to fight treachery in Rome. As it was, Mithradates and his allies had to pay an immense fine. But at least he survived, and went on to tweak the lion's tail several times more during his long and violent reign.

His end has a certain grim irony. His luck and cunning had outwitted many assassination attempts, but he became so afraid of assassination that he made a habit of taking small doses of poison to immunise himself against it. Finally, after slaughtering dozens of his relatives — on suspicion of plotting against him — as well as several of his wives and children, he realised that his luck was running out when his son Pharaces led an army revolt against him. Knowing he could expect no mercy from his own flesh and blood, Mithradates tried to poison himself, but seemed immune to everything he swallowed. Finally,

Alexander the Great

in desperation, he had to ask a member of his own bodyguard run him through with a sword.

The First Spy-Master

At the time he committed suicide, Mithradates was being pursued by a Roman general called Pompey, and it is Pompey who brings us to our next chapter in the history of spying. For Pompey's two closest allies in Rome were a brilliant young soldier called Julius Caesar, and a millionaire named Marcus Crassus, who has the interesting distinction of being the world's first spymaster, as well as the inventor of the protection racket.

As a young man, Crassus had survived one of Rome's periodic purges by escaping to Spain and hiding in a seaside cave. He was broke — the market crash caused by a civil war having bankrupted his family — and decided to became a Mediterranean pirate, which was at the time a fairly easy — if brutal and horrible — way of making a living. After plundering a town called Malaca, he raised enough money to buy a fleet of ships, which he offered to General Sulla — the man who had defeated Mithradates — and who was now dictator of Rome. Together with Pompey Crassus was soon one of Sulla's favourites.

Crassus then proceeded to make a fortune by buying-up the property of proscribed (i.e. executed or exiled) Romans at rock bottom prices, and quickly became one of the richest men in Rome. It helped to reconcile him to not being as fine a soldier as Pompey, who was soon known as 'the Great'.

Putting his money to work, Crassus became the premier money-lender in the city. No matter how much was asked for, Crassus could finance it; generally at a very high interest rate. Inevitably, many citizens found themselves in debt to him. Depending on their influence, he either squeezed them for every penny he could get, or made a deal with them – a reduction on the interest payments in return for unconditional support when he asked for it. The very powerful or influential were not charged interest at all. Crassus merely made sure they understood that they owed him a favour or two.

Most wealthy Romans invested their money in estates and corn shipments. Crassus, with the true instinct of an entrepreneur, aimed at totally new areas of the market. For example, he built an educational academy for slaves. Up to that point, most slaves were illiterate and devoid of all but the simplest skills. 'Graduates' from Crassus' school soon commanded the highest prices, and became a status symbol among the Roman elite.

Using five hundred slaves from his own academy, he now set up the world's first fire brigade. The crowded streets of Rome were full of houses of all shapes and sizes, which were built from rough daub bricks and wood (it was not until the days of the Emperor Augustus that Rome was 'dressed in marble'). Open fires and the use of torches meant that they were always bursting into flame. Often whole neighbourhoods burned down within hours.

As soon as they heard of a blaze, Crassus' fire brigade – often led by the great man himself – would hurry to the site of the tragedy, armed with ropes, ladders, buckets and demolition tools. When they arrived, they noted the wind direction, and went to all endangered households with an offer to purchase at well below the market value. If the homeowners sold to Crassus, his slaves would swing into action, quenching the blaze with professional expertise. On the other hand, if not enough householders made it worth his while, Crassus would turn his men about and march them home, leaving the locals to deal with the problem. Using these methods – which might fairly be described as a protection racket – Crassus soon owned a large proportion of all the property in Rome. He also became the first self-made multi-millionaire in history.

But Crassus realised that his wealth aroused envy, and that he had hundreds of enemies who were plotting his downfall. The best way to guard against this was to organise a network of spies and informers. To begin with, there were the slaves who had graduated from his academy – Crassus would pay well for useful titbits of information overheard at the dinner table. Then there were all the citizens who owed him money or favours, and who could buy his patience by telling him who was plotting against him. His contacts were always ready to pass on secret information concerning the markets, so we might also add the title first insider-dealer to his list of dubious achievements. Crassus prided himself with being the best-informed man in the city.

Inevitably, Crassus spent a great deal of his time in court, defending himself against charges of fraud and deceit. His spy network meant that he seldom lost a case. Where other men would try to sway the judges with fine rhetoric, Crassus would come to court armed with piles of evidence and information, which he sprayed against his opponents like shotgun pellets. The judges preferred facts to rhetoric, and usually awarded Crassus the case – although it probably also helped that most of the judges owed him a favour or two.

It was Crassus' thirst for military glory that was to be his downfall. His friend Pompey had defeated Mithradates and cleared the pirates out of the Mediterranean in one powerful and ruthless military operation. As a result, he was called Pompey the Great, while Rome's only multi-millionaire was merely Crassus the Rich. Then Crassus got his chance to prove that he was also a great general.

When a gang of highly trained slaves escaped from a gladiator school and started a slave revolt in southern Italy, the Romans were first more indignant than frightened. It was only when the slaves, under a Thessalian gladiator called Spartacus, defeated an avenging Roman army, that the citizens began to worry. Pompey was away in Spain at the time, and Crassus sensed an easy victory. Using his enormous influence and wealth, he persuaded the Senate to give him command of the second expedition against Spartacus. He then marched south to Mount Vesuvius — where the rebel slaves were based — and, after a desperate battle, defeated them. (The relieved people of Rome had the 6,000 prisoners captured by Crassus crucified to a man.) Even then, Pompey managed to steal his victory from under his nose. Hurrying back from Spain, he managed to mop-up a few rebel stragglers and beat Crassus to Rome. As a result, it was Pompey who was awarded a full triumph for his Spanish victory, while Crassus had to make-do with a smaller celebration.

Instead of brooding on his injuries, Crassus went into partnership with Pompey, and with another popular Roman named Julius Caesar — not then a military hero, but a favourite with the Roman public because he was always putting on free entertainments (with money borrowed from Crassus). Together, the millionaire, the war hero and man-of-the-people dubbed themselves the Triumvirate, while their enemies nervously referred to them as 'the three-headed monster'. United, they were an almost unstoppable political force — Pompey's military prestige, Caesar's popularity, and Crassus's unmatched information network. Very soon the three of them ruled Rome in all but name.

Yet as Caesar also became a famous general, Crassus yearned for the laurels of the conqueror. Caesar had conquered Gaul, Pompey had conquered North Africa; he would outshine them both by conquering the Parthian empire to the east — in fact, by marching his troops as far as India.

In 203 BC, Rome was engaged in a long-standing war with their trading competitor, Carthage. In North Africa the brilliant Roman General Scipio Africanus was facing an ally of Carthage, King Syphax of Numidia. Unfortunately for the Romans, Syphax and his army were an unknown quantity; Scipio had no idea of his enemy's numbers, tactics or defences. The obvious answer was espionage.

The Romans called for a armistice and offered to send a peace delegation of civilians to the Numidian camp. Syphax agreed, but remained highly suspicious. He ruled that none of the delegates was to leave an enclosed compound in the middle of his camp. They were to be transported there blindfolded.

A Roman commander called Laelius proposed a way around the problem. He and his men disguised themselves as the delegate's slaves, hoping that they would be allowed to run errands around the camp while attention rested on their 'masters'. To add to the realism of the plot, the delegates were told to occasionally beat the spies – an indignity suffered regularly by slaves, but unheard of for a Roman officer.

The ruse, unfortuntely, seemed a failure. The 'slaves' were held in the compound with the delegates and not allowed out. Finally, on the last day of the talks, Laelius tried a desperate plan. He and his fellow agents deliberately panicked their horses and – pretending to be trying to catch them – chased them out of the

> compound and all around the Numidian camp.
> By the time they had caught the animals, the
> spies had all the information they needed.

His first step was to use his money and influence to become governor of Syria. But at this point, he forgot the lessons he had learned as the best-informed man in Rome: that victory usually goes to the person with the best intelligence network. If he had sent out spies to learn the strength and weakness of the enemy, he would have discovered that Roman foot-soldiers were no match for Parthian horsemen, who had the skill of circus riders, and could fire accurately from the back of a galloping horse; moreover, their horn bows could penetrate Roman armour from a long distance. When Crassus led his army across the Euphrates, he was virtually committing suicide. The Parthian horsemen surrounded the Romans and slaughtered them in their thousands. The heavily armoured Roman soldiers did their best to get close to the enemy, but the Parthians galloped around them and picked them off at their leisure. Defeated and captured, Crassus was beheaded, and his mouth filled with molten gold. So history's first spymaster brought about his own downfall by forgetting that a little accurate information is worth a dozen regiments.

Macchiavelli

We have already observed that spying depends on deceit and betrayal. All modern governments use it; none would be willing to defend it on moral grounds. So a book called *The Prince*, which appeared in 1613, is a kind of landmark in human history, for it recommends blackmail, murder, torture and betrayal without any attempt at apology. Its author, Niccolo Macchiavelli, deserves an honourable mention in any history of spying.

He was a native of the city of Florence. Born into an impoverished family – his father was an embittered treasury official who had lost most of his money – Macchiavelli was determined to make good, no matter what it cost. When he was twenty-five – in 1494 – he saw the downfall of the Medici family, after which Florence was taken over by the puritanical monk Savonarola, who made women throw their jewellery and silk dresses into a bonfire; four years later, Macchiavelli saw the monk tortured and hanged, after which his body was burned on the spot where he had lit the 'bonfire of the vanities'.

For a while, Florence became a republic, and Macchiavelli became a political secretary. His masters soon recognised his astuteness, and sent him on 'diplomatic' missions. In fact, he became a spy, sending back intelligence reports from every important city state in Italy, and many outside it.

The man who had ordered Savonarola's arrest was Pope Rodrigo Borgia, probably the most corrupt and debauched pope in the history of the Church. It was his son, Cesare Borgia, who became Macchiavelli's hero. When Macchiavelli met him, Borgia had already murdered his brother, impregnated his sister, murdered his sister's husband, and conquered most of the area called Romagna.

Macchiavelli was dazzled by Cesare's brutality, ruthlessness and cunning. He was particularly impressed by one masterstroke of treachery. Romagna was a poverty-stricken area, which had been devastated by war so often that most of its inhabitants had turned to banditry. The only way to restore law and order was with a certain amount of brutality. But if he applied too much brutality, the peasants might revolt, and he would be worse off than before. So he appointed the most ruthless and brutal man he knew –

Niccolo Macchiavelli, author of *The Prince*

Remirro de Orca — to restore law and order. Orca was a sadist who enjoyed causing terror, and he soon had the whole region cowering. At that point, Cesare Borgia went to inspect Orca's work, and pretended to be appalled by his excesses. To rousing cheers from the populace, he had Orca arrested, and sliced in two in the public square of Cesena. So he achieved his two aims — popularity *and* law and order.

Macchiavelli also watched with approval when Cesare Borgia decided to get rid of enemies who were plotting against his life. He charmed the plotters — all noblemen — with offers of good will and future alliances. Then he invited them all to dinner. As they sat down to the banquet, they were seized from behind and strangled.

When Pope Borgia died in 1503, Cesare knew his career was over. He was arrested, escaped, then arrested again on the orders of the widow of his murdered brother. In 1507 he was wounded in battle and died of thirst.

Seven years later, Macchiavelli's political career came to an abrupt end when the Medici's were restored to power in Florence. They were, in effect, its royal family, and Macchiavelli had been the servant of their enemies. He was arrested and tortured, but finally released. At the age of forty-three he retired to his small farm near Florence. Now he was no longer in politics he felt like a fish out of water. He loved the exercise of power, and he loved to study power. So he did the next best thing — he began to write about power. He wrote *The Prince*, the first realistic treatise on politics.

What he wanted, of course, was to be taken back. He hoped that the men in power — in Rome as well as Florence — would recognise that he would make an ideal tool. *The Prince* had the reverse effect; with its pungent cynicism it made him dozens of enemies. He was still living in hope when he died at the age of fifty-eight. And ever since then, the word 'Macchiavellian' has meant cunning, deceitful, crafty, unscrupulous and treacherous.

Was he really as black as he was painted? His defenders say that he only wanted to see Italy united under one ruler, and that he realised that such a ruler would have to be as cunning and heartless as a weasel. He was not treacherous — just realistic.

That may or may not be true. What is undoubtedly true is that these Macchiavellian weasels make the best spy-masters.

Spying became the official policy of the British government in the 1460, when King Edward IV introduced what he called 'the King's espials'. In those days it was regarded as an honourable branch of international diplomacy. In the reign of Queen Elizabeth I, her Lord Treasurer Burghley controlled one of the most powerful intelligence networks in Europe. Oddly enough, one of his spies was the Elizabethan playwright Christopher Marlowe, who died mysteriously in a tavern brawl in May 1593, near the beginning of a career that might have made him as great as Shakespeare. One Elizabethan historian, Calvin Hoffmann, is even convinced that Marlowe *was* Shakespeare. Marlowe died just as Shakespeare's career was beginning, and the style of the early Shakespeare plays is certainly very much like Marlowe's. In *The Murder of the Man called Shakespeare*, Hoffmann advances the astonishing theory that Marlowe 'died' with the aid of his espionage boss, Sir Francis Walshinghame, then continued his existence under another name — Shakespeare. The theory has never been widely accepted by scholars, but Hoffmann has produced some convincing evidence in its favour.

Daniel Defoe

The man who taught Englishmen to spy on one another was a true Macchiavellian. His name was Daniel Foe, but we know him better as Daniel Defoe, the author of *Robinson Crusoe*. In fact, Defoe was one of the greatest scoundrels and cheats who ever became a literary classic. Not that he ever committed any real crimes, like murder or highway robbery – he was far too wily for that. But in his lifetime of seventy years he lied, cheated and swindled with a vitality and effrontery that should have made him a millionaire. Instead, he died in an obscure lodging house, fleeing from his creditors.

Daniel Foe was born in London in 1660, the son of a butcher of St Giles, Cripplegate. His family were 'dissenters', that is, nonconformists who disagreed with Catholicism and Protestantism. Foe was so much a dissenter that in 1683, at the age of twenty-three, he enraged his fellow dissenters by publishing a pamphlet in which he said the Turks had no business besieging Vienna (as they were now doing under the leadership of Kara Mustapha), and that he hoped they wouldn't succeed, even if the Viennese *were* Catholics. In 1685, Foe was involved in the Duke of Monmouth's rebellion against James II and was lucky to avoid being condemned to death by the sadistic Judge Jeffreys. He married well – the lady brought him a dowry of £3,700 – set up in business as a wholesaler of stockings, and made a quick fortune. Extravagance and bad management led to bankruptcy, and he was forced to flee from his creditors. He went to Bristol, where he became known as 'the Sunday gentleman', that being the only day he dared to venture out of his lodgings without fear of arrest. By this time, William of Orange was on the throne of England. 'Dutch Billy' was not a popular king; he was a lonely, introverted man who seemed to have a knack of getting himself disliked.

The poet Dryden was offered a large sum of money to dedicate his translation of Virgil's *Aeneid* to the king, but preferred to issue it without a dedication. But Daniel Foe saw his chance and offered his services to the government as a pamphleteer. The first result was a tract, issued in 1694, defending the unpopular war with France, which William was losing, 'and serving King William and Queen Mary and acknowledging their Right'. William, whose popularity was lower than usual because of the treacherous massacre of the MacDonalds at Glencoe, was glad of a supporter, and Foe was given a profitable government post. He also took advantage of the new fashion for Dutch tiles to start a tile factory at Tilbury, and was finally able to pay off all his creditors.

In 1701, Foe issued a poem called *The True Born Englishman*, which enjoyed enormous success; its argument was that it was unfair to abuse Dutch Billy for being a foreigner, since all Englishmen are a compound of nationalities — Celts, Saxons, Vikings, Normans and Picts. Unfortunately, William of Orange died in the following year, and Foe found himself temporarily without a patron.

In *The True Born Englishman* he sneers at people who pretend their family came over with William the Conqueror. But shortly thereafter he began signing himself D. Foe, then De Foe, then Daniel De Foe. When he next came to public notice, a year later, he was Daniel Defoe. The occasion was a pamphlet called *The Shortest Way With Dissenters*, although this was not actually signed. Under William of Orange, dissenters had been allowed to hold public office, provided they were willing to pay occasional lip-service to Anglicanism. After the king's death, reactionaries — known as 'high fliers' because of their high principles — began to demand that dissenters should be banned from public office. Oddly enough, Defoe agreed with the high fliers; he thought the kind of dissenters who were willing to compromise were a poor lot. His pamphlet satirized the high fliers by suggesting that all dissenters should be banished or hanged. It was rather as if an American liberal wrote a book suggesting that all negroes should be sent back to Africa, and that those who refused to go should be burned alive, and signed it with the name of some well-known reactionary. Many high fliers were taken in and greeted the pamphlet with enthusiasm – one clergyman said he valued it above all books except the Bible, and prayed that Queen Anne would carry out its suggestions. The dissenters were at first terrified – haunted by visions of being burnt at the stake. Then it leaked out that this was one of Defoe's hard-hitting jokes, and everyone was furious. Parliament issued a warrant for Defoe's arrest on a charge of libelling the high fliers by making them out to be bloodthirsty maniacs. Defoe went into hiding and tried to apologize, but it was no good; he had to give himself up. In July 1703, he was sentenced to stand in the pillory for three days and to be detained during the queen's pleasure.

It was, in fact, his best stroke of luck so far. Overnight, he became a popular hero. The crowds who gathered at the pillory shouted 'Good old Dan' and threw bunches of flowers. There would be nothing like it for another fifty years, when John Wilkes would find himself a popular hero through a similar accident.

Defoe was then confined in Newgate for a year, where he mingled with pickpockets and footpads – accumulating material for future novels – and continued to write pamphlets. He was now so popular that no government could silence him. He started his first newspaper in jail – it was called *The Review* and was full of political commentary, lively interviews with thieves and murderers, and gossip about current scandals. He was becoming a power with his pen.

He obtained his freedom by approaching the Lord Treasurer with a scheme that was worthy of Machiavelli. He suggested that the government needed a network of informers to point out potential critics and enemies: in short, an army of spies. The Lord Treasurer was just the man to approach with such a sinister idea; Robert Harley was a born schemer, a man of whom a contemporary wrote: 'He loved tricks, even where not necessary, but from an inward satisfaction he took in applauding his own cunning. If any man was ever born under the necessity of being a knave, he was.' It is a description that applies equally well to Defoe.

The result was that Queen Anne was prevailed upon to release Defoe from prison, and Defoe proceeded to travel the country and build up a network of agents. It would hardly be an exaggeration to call him the father of the police state. He laid down the basic rules for spying. Each agent had to appear to be an ordinary citizen; every one had to be unknown to the others. The aim was unobtrusive thought-control of the people of England. And the scheme was amazingly successful — in fact, Defoe's network became the foundation of the British Secret Service. And he quickly established its value by playing a significant part in the union of England and Scotland into one country called Great Britain. The English liked the idea; the Scots were dubious. Defoe went off to Scotland in 1706, with half a dozen plausible cover stories — that he was a ship-builder, a wool merchant, a fish merchant, and so on. He became intimate with various government ministers in Scotland, and quietly influenced opinion. In May 1707, Scotland and England became Great Britain, and Defoe returned home well satisfied.

In 1710, the Whig (i.e. liberal) government fell; Defoe, who had made his reputation as a fighter for liberal principles, quickly switched sides, declaring, with his usual glibness, that he cared more for his country than for party prejudice. But in 1714, Harley — who had become an alcoholic — was dismissed; Queen Anne died a few days later, and a Whig administration came into power under George I. Defoe was thrown into prison, and although he obtained his freedom, he was soon back in jail again on a charge of libelling the Earl of Anglesey. Once again, he offered his services as a spy. And the Whigs, who knew his abilities, decided that a discredited Tory might make an excellent spy — particularly if everyone assumed he was still in disgrace. He might, as an 'enemy' of the government, find out what their opponents were planning. And at the moment, their opponents were not the Tories so much as the Jacobites — supporters of the house of Stuart. Under the guise of a government opponent, Defoe gained the confidence of various anti-government newspapers, and was soon using his Machiavellian skills to suppress anything the government disliked.

Sooner or later, he was bound to be found out. One of his dupes was a man called Mist, who ran a Jacobite newspaper. Mist printed a letter criticizing the government without showing it to Defoe, and when he was summoned before government ministers tried to put the blame on Defoe. The Whigs began to suspect that Defoe was doubly treacherous. The breach was healed, but Defoe seems to have realized that his days as a double-dealer were numbered. He had to find some other way of making a living. He recollected that he possessed the material for an interesting narrative. In 1704, a Scottish pirate named Alexander Selkirk had quarrelled with his pirate captain and been marooned, at his own request, on an uninhabited island called Juan Fernandez. He spent five years there before he was rescued, and when he returned to England, became a celebrity. Defoe probably went to see him in Bristol in

Daniel Defoe

1713, and bought his papers for a trifling sum. Using this material as a basis, Defoe dashed off *Robinson Crusoe*. The book appeared in 1719, and immediately became a classic. Unfortunately for Defoe, it instantly appeared in several pirated editions, so he made less from it than he might. But he went on to write more novels – *Captain Singleton, Moll Flanders, Colonel Jack, Journal of the Plague Year* and others. By the early 1720s, his credit as a spy had collapsed completely, and he lived mainly from his novels. But these were highly popular – particularly novels of 'low life' like *Moll Flanders*, which may well have inspired Osborn to bring out his *Lives of the Notorious Criminals*. His end was typical. In August 1730, at the age of seventy, he suddenly disappeared. Until recently, the reason has been a mystery, but research has revealed that old debts – his tile factory had gone bankrupt while he was in prison for his dissenters pamphlet – were catching up with him. He could almost certainly have paid them off with the money from his novels. Instead, he preferred to abscond again. He died in the April of the following year in an obscure lodging house, not far from the spot where he was born.

Spies in the New World

During the American War of Independence, there were some notable spying exploits. Nathan Hale, spying for the Americans, was captured and executed in the first year of the war. He died saying, 'I only regret that I have but one life to lose for my country' – the kind of sentiment that would make a modern spy snort cynically. Hale became a martyr; so did the British spy, Major John André, carrying messages to the infamous traitor Benedict Arnold. Women spies also came into their own during the War of Independence, since no one could tell *which* side a woman belonged to, and the officers of both sides were far too gallant to search a woman. Belle Boyd, a 'rebel' spy, had Northern officers quartered in her house in Martinsburg, Virginia, so was able to gather all kinds of information about troop movements, which she promptly relayed to Stonewall Jackson. (On one famous occasion, she got through the Northern lines and delivered a message that enabled Stonewall Jackson to win an important battle.) The most amusing thing about her career is that the Northern officers were soon convinced she was a spy, but were forbidden by chivalry to take any action. She *was* finally arrested, when one of her despatches fell into the hands of a Union agent, but she was exchanged for a Northern prisoner, and became a heroine in the South. The careers of 'Rebel Rose' Greenhow and Pauline Cushman (a spy for the North) were equally remarkable, and have become a part of American folklore.

Wilhelm Stieber – Germany's First Spy-Master

The German Kaiser Wilhelm I was another of the old school who thought that spying was '*infra dig*'. When he became Kaiser in 1861 he had in his service one of the most brilliant spy-masters in Europe – in fact, the man who virtually turned spying into an art form. Few people nowadays have heard of Wilhelm Stieber, yet he holds a central place in the history of espionage.

When Wilhelm Johann Carl Eduard Stieber was born in Prussian Saxony in 1818, Germany was as politically fragmented as Italy in Machiavelli's time. The country was split between the Prussians and the semi-independent trading cities of the north, while the French, Russian and Austrian empires were a constant threat to everybody. Stieber helped to change all that.

Spies

The son of a minor government official, Stieber trained as a Lutheran preacher, then as a lawyer. After qualifying, he moved to Berlin and worked in the police courts, defending petty crooks. This was not because he sympathised with the oppressed, but because, being naturally devious, he wanted to place himself in a position where he could act as a police spy. While he defended his clients in court, and gained the trust of the underworld, he informed against them behind their backs. Stieber was a born worshipper of authority. By the age of 27, he was accepted by liberals as one of themselves when he was actually a leading police informer and *agent provocateur*. He even denounced his wife's uncle as a dangerous radical.

In the mid 1840's, Prussia was in political turmoil — partly because of the weakness of its Hohenzollern ruler, Friedrich Wilhelm IV, a romantic liberal who lived in permanent terror of the mob. During the political disturbances in 1848, the king unaccountably found himself separated from his bodyguard and confronted by a street full of angry Berlin citizens. They recognised him and shouted rude names. Then as the cowering monarch looked desperately for an escape route, he suddenly found himself face to face with the well-known liberal lawyer Wilhelm Stieber.

In fact, Stieber was working on behalf of the political police, addressing treasonable words to the mob in the hope of making them do something rash and provoking mass arrests. He was momentarily taken by surprise by the arrival of King Friedrich Wilhelm. Pulling himself together, he stepped forward, as if to speak on behalf of the mob, and whispered in the King's ear that he could protect him provided he tried to appear friendly and showed no fear. Taking him by the arm he led the monarch through the crowd who, being mostly middle-class shop keepers, had no intention of harming him anyway. Friedrich Wilhelm,

24

however, was not astute enough to recognise this, and after crushing the revolution, he showed his gratitude to Stieber by becoming his patron.

Stieber used his new influence to enrich his legal practice. He was given full access to the files of the political police and found he could study the prosecution's case before he and his client appeared in court. Naturally, his defence tactics were brilliantly well-informed, and every weak-point in the prosecution's case was exploited. He even seemed to know in advance about 'surprise witnesses'. By 1850, he had successfully defended over 3,000 clients, becoming in the process one of the heroes of the Berlin underworld.

His success, of course, depended on playing a double game. Respected equally by professional criminals and radical activists, Stieber was in an ideal position to inform on any unlawful of subversive activity. For every criminal he helped to acquit, he probably betrayed two or three.

In a mere two years, Friedrich Wilhelm had Stieber appointed Commissioner of Police. But the promotion was not publicised. Its purpose was bring him into the fold as a salaried employee, and allow him to use police manpower as and when he wanted. In all probability, this was Stieber's idea; the thirty-two year old lawyer could see that his royal benefactor was rapidly going insane. When the time came for Friedrich Wilhelm to abdicate, Stieber wanted to hold a reasonably secure place in the administration.

His first mission abroad took him to London, where a Jewish left-wing agitator had fled from Germany; now he had settled in Soho, and was churning-out extremist pamphlets which were all the rage in Berlin's radical underground. This political undesirable, whose name was Karl Marx, was rumoured to be writing a book which advocated violent revolution by the working classes, the eradication of the class system, an end to religion and the sharing-out of all property. Indeed, Marx seemed to want to undermine everything Stieber held dear. The task of persuading the British authorities to either hand Marx to the Prussian secret police or arrest him themselves must have been one Stieber relished.

He sailed to England under the guise of a tourist going to see the Great Exhibition. At Scotland Yard, Stieber revealed himself as an official of the Berlin police and asked what had been done to muzzle the revolutionary. To his dismay, he was told that the British authorities did not consider Marx a threat. While he refrained from trying to start a revolution in Great Britain or her dominions, he was welcome to write what he liked. The worst he was likely to do was start a fist-fight in the British Museum Reading Room. Baffled and irritated by British tolerance and complacency, Stieber could only record the whereabouts and activities of Marx and his disciples, and hope that he would be rash enough to return to Berlin.

He had more luck in Paris – another hotbed of exiled German radicals and socialists. Posing as a fellow liberal, Stieber infiltrated their circles and told everyone how worried he was to be going back to Germany in a few weeks. Concerned for a fellow comrade, many gave him the names and addresses of friends and relatives in Germany who would help if he was in need. Shortly after his return to Berlin, a wave of arrests snatched-up everyone on his list.

This was just the beginning. Over the next eight years Stieber conducted a personal crusade to drive liberal thought from German soil. His efforts led to an exodus of free-thinkers which, while enriching the intellectual life of more tolerant countries like Britain and America, left a hard-core of extreme die-hards and revolutionaries in Germany.

The Trade of Treachery

The master-spy was not himself as secure as he would have liked. In 1858, just as Stieber was preparing to have himself elected to the Prussian Parliament to infiltrate the liberals there, Friedrich Wilhelm went completely mad. His family had no choice but to persuade him to abdicate, and place him in the care of his doctors. The new ruler, Kaiser Wilhelm I, owed Stieber nothing and looked upon his covert activities with extreme distaste. The once influential spy found himself defenceless against his many enemies. He was first sacked, then arrested and brought to trial, charged with activities against the state. A lawyer through and through, Stieber had long been prepared for such an eventuality. He presented indisputable evidence that everything he had done had been approved by the monarch, and therefore could not, by definition, be treasonable. He was acquitted, but his cover as a liberal figurehead was thoroughly blown, and he had become one of the most hated men in Prussia. The liberals were delighted to see him get his come-uppance.

Oddly enough, it was the fact that his activities were now public knowledge that won him his next espionage position. The tsarist government in Russia was having its own problem with liberals and revolutionaries. Stieber was invited to take part in setting up a secret police bureau to be called the Okhrana. During the next five year, Stieber played a major part in creating an organisation so effective that its basic structure survived a hundred and twenty-five years and four name changes – from the Okhrana to the Cheka, then the GPU, then the NKVD, and finally the KGB.

The Russian government trusted Stieber because, during his days of power in Berlin, he had gone out of his way to suppress a scandal involving a Russian diplomat's wife; this was their mistake. Although Stieber respected the Russians because they were ruled by an absolute monarch, he never forgot his loyalty to his own country. Throughout his years in St. Petersburg, he collected secret military information and sent it home to Berlin – strengthening his position with the administration that had tried to jail him.

During his time in St Petersburg, Stieber was introduced to the young Prussian Ambassador, the Graf von Bismarck. By 1863, soon after Stieber returned to Berlin, Bismark had effectively seized control of the enfeebled Prussian government. The man who would come to be known as the Iron Chancellor was determined to unify all the German states under the Prussian flag. To do this, he realised, he would need the help of an experienced spy-master. Stieber was the obvious choice.

Bismark's first objective, he explained to Stieber, was the humbling of Imperial Austria. The Hapsburg empire had stood in the way of German unification for centuries. Now they were becoming decadent, but they still had a formidable army. Bismark needed to know exactly how effective it was. Stieber was given a generous budget and carte blanche to recruit informants. But he decided to make the initial observations himself.

Disguised as a seller of holy statues ('blessed by the Pope himself') and pornographic drawings, he wandered about Austria gathering information. The dirty postcards were a brilliant idea. They got him into endless discussions in bierkellers with young soldiers, and explained why he was so anxious to avoid contact with the police. The holy statues provided an excuse to strike up conversations with soldiers' wives about where their husbands were stationed. When, at the end of two years, he presented his findings to the Commander in Chief von Moltke, they were so incredibly detailed that the general at first suspected that they were pure invention. But Bismarck knew better – he liked to refer to Stieber as 'the king of the sleuth hounds'.

The Austro-Prussian war of 1866 was one of the swiftest and most decisive of modern times. In 45 days, Prussia's troops smashed Austrian resistance. Bismarck was well satisfied; he was not looking for territorial gains – only the end of Austrian meddling in German affairs. The swiftness of the campaign was due basically to Stieber's stolen information.

Even Kaiser Wilhelm warmed to Stieber after Bismark sang his praises, and publicly admitted that Stieber's trial and unofficial exile had been a 'bureaucratic error'. Stieber was promoted to the rank of Privy Councillor. But the generals were less enthusiastic – Bismark eventually had to order von Moltke to present Stieber with a medal, and even then, the Commander-in-Chief publicly apologised to his staff for lowering the tone of the decoration.

Unperturbed by these snubs, Stieber devoted himself to creating a German secret police network like the Okhrana. Army movements were declared top secret, and peasants ordered, on pain of death, to close their shutters when troops passed through town. Stieber's network of spies reported all suspicious behaviour, including people who peeped through the curtain at passing soldiers. Since no agent knew the identity of any other agent, this occasionally led to Stieber's own informants being accused and executed, but he considered this a small price to pay for national security. He also organised a disinformation service, disguised as an independent news bureau, that confused the whole of Europe about Prussia's strength and intentions. Joseph Goebbels was later responsible for the term 'the Big Lie', but it was Stieber who first put the concept into practice

Bismarck's next priority aim was to humble the French, but he was deterred by their pact with Russia. Stieber solved the problem with characteristic cunning. Tsar Alexander II happened to be in Paris when Stieber's agents reported a plot to kill the monarch was being hatched by Russian exiles. The assassination was to take place on a fixed date – at a military review – and Stieber knew the names of all the principal plotters. But if he informed the French authorities, the conspirators would be quietly arrested, and no one would ever hear about it. Stieber decided to withhold the information until the day before the assassination attempt.

As Stieber had expected, the French panicked. The review was called-off and the tsar hastily bundled out of his luxury hotel to a place of safety. Alexander was delighted with their efficiency. But when he learned that the French were not going to execute the plotters, or even put them on trial, he was baffled and infuriated. His hosts expressed their regret, but explained that the would-be assassins had been arrested before they could commit a felony and, under French law, the worst the authorities could do was deport them. The tsar, used to a more medieval system of justice, left France in a purple rage and diplomatic relations between Russia and France cooled to near freezing-point.

Shortly thereafter, Stieber slipped into France himself to steal the plans of the French army's new mitrailleuse – an early type of machine-gun, and at the same time assessed the military capabilities of the French army. He was glad to report that France was torn by internal strife and without effective political leadership. (The situation would repeat itself in 1940.) Bismarck immediately ordered the army to prepare to invade. In the few months before the declaration of war, no less than 40,000 of Stieber's agents succeeded in infiltrating Alsace, in eastern France. No French unit could move a mile down the road without the Germans knowing about it. The Franco-Prussian war of 1870 was as short and decisive as the Austro-Prussian war, and ended in total French humiliation.

During the peace negotiations at Versailles, Stieber succeeded in getting himself employed as valet to the principal French negotiator. Whenever he was left alone,

Stieber ransacked the diplomat's papers and sent detailed reports to Bismarck. As a result, Bismarck's diplomatic offensive was as successful as the war he had just won. Shortly thereafter, Kaiser Wilhelm was crowned Emperor Wilhelm I of the newly declared German Empire.

In his later years, Stieber confined his activities to Berlin. His favourite method of checkmating his opponents was blackmail. They were lured to a brothel called the Green House, which offered its clients a staggering range of perversions. Politicians, diplomats, aristocrats and even lesser royalty – from both Germany and abroad – were induced to accept its hospitality, then gently persuaded into working for Stieber's information network.

The master spy remained in office more than fifty years, and retired, loaded with decorations, to a large estate. There he wrote his memoirs, and died in 1892, the only penalty visited upon him by fate for a lifetime of deceit and treachery being the painful arthritis that incapacitated him in his last years. His espionage network was still flourishing at the outbreak of the Great War.

Colonel Alfred Redl

As we shall see, the First World War would form a watershed in the history of espionage. Before that spying had been an altogether more gentlemanly business. In fact, in the last great European spy case before the war, the traitor had been allowed to borrow a revolver and shoot himself through the head to avoid scandal. Colonel Alfred Redl's treason probably cost his country a quarter of a million lives.

Redl was a highly intelligent man who came from a poor family. He was also a homosexual. In the Austria of the nineteenth century, the army offered a certain mode of advancement to one of Redl's character. In the early years of the century, his rise was rapid. His intelligence brought him to the attention of Baron von Giesl, head of the Austro-Hungarian intelligence service. He placed the young officer in charge of espionage, hardly an important activity in that rather old fashioned, militaristic nation. But Redl proved to be brilliant. He had the kind of imagination that would have taken him far in the CIA. He learned to use hidden cameras to photograph unsuspecting visitors; he coated objects with a fine dust, to get their fingerprints; he made recordings of their conversations (on old Edison cylinders). For the first decade of the twentieth century, he was a high-powered spy.

Unfortunately, he lived in a country where homosexuality was regarded as pure, deliberate wickedness. In the drawing rooms where the elegant and witty Colonel Redl was a welcome guest, any suspicion of his sexual tastes would have been enough to ruin him. It was necessary for him to be discreet. And since his sexual appetite was strong, this meant that, like Oscar Wilde, he had to be prepared to pay male prostitutes. It was an expensive business.

A Russian secret agent got wind of Redl's secret. And sometime around the year 1903, he informed Redl that if he wanted his secret to be kept, it would be necessary to aid the Russian secret service in certain minor matters. No one knows the details. All that is certain is that a combination of blackmail and bribery turned Redl into a traitor.

Von Giesl moved to Prague, and Redl went with him. His place in Vienna was taken by an adoring disciple, Captain Maximilian Ronge. Ronge was not a brilliant innovator, like Redl, but he was painstaking and precise. One of Redl's ideas was the institution of strict postal censorship; Ronge made sure it was carried out thoroughly. And in 1913, in the course of routine inspection, one of his agents came across two *post restante* letters, addressed simply to 'Opera

In the seventeenth century, the greatest spy-master in Europe was Cardinal Richelieu of France. Richelieu, immortalised as the villain of Alexander Dumas' *The Three Musketeers*, spread a web of agents across the continent which would have been the envy of any twentieth century superpower. Working with his right-hand man – a Capuchin monk named Father Joseph, nervously referred to by friend and enemy alike as 'the Grey Eminence' – Richelieu engineered revolutions in North Africa, Portugal, Spain and the Austrian Empire. He turned the Protestant champion Gustavus Adolphus against his Hapsburg patrons; thwarted the designs of the Duke of Buckingham, the ambitious British Prime Minister; and kept France out of the disastrous Thirty Years War, which was ruining the economies of other leading European states.

For the eighteen years he was First Minister, Richelieu used his network of informers to rule France with an iron hand. It was said of him that he believed civil disobedience to be a sin against God. His skill as a politician, both open and covert, led his country to a position of pre-eminence, but his harsh internal measures created the misery which would eventually lead to the French Revolution. Ironically, after the Cardinal's death, Louis XIV converted his complex spying organisation into France's first police force.

Ball 13'. Both envelopes contained fairly large sums of money. Ronge ordered his agents to watch the post office and see who came for the envelopes. They waited for weeks in the police station next door, waiting for the ringing of a bell that would tell them that the letters were being collected. One day, it rang. They rushed next door in time to see a taxi vanishing. They managed to trace the cab to a hotel; there they were told their quarry had taken a cab to another hotel, the Klomser. And on the cab seat, one of the agents picked up a small suede sheath, of the sort that contained nail clippers. He asked the clerk at the Klomser if he knew the owner of the sheath. The clerk took it and approached a good-looking man of military bearing. The man nodded and slipped the sheath into his pocket. It was Colonel Redl.

One agent shadowed Redl, the other telephoned Ronge. Ronge was shattered. It was surely impossible that the ex-head of the Secret Service could be a traitor! He got hold of the receipts that Redl had signed to get the letters, and compared them with some of Redl's own handwriting in the files. They were identical. By this time, Redl had noticed that he was being followed. He did a stupid thing. He had some incriminating receipts in his pocket, for money from Russia. He tore these into small pieces, and cautiously scattered them as he walked. But Ronge's agents had been trained in Redl's own counter-espionage methods; they collected every tiny fragment and took them to Ronge's office.

Ronge went to the Commander-in-Chief of the army. He was stunned by the possibility that Redl might have been an enemy agent for years. For Austria had plans for attacking Russia and the Balkans, particularly Serbia. Redl had access to these papers, known collectively as Plan Three.

The Austrians behaved like gentlemen, which was their mistake. They called on Redl at his hotel and laid the facts before him. Redl looked pale and composed. He told them that they would find all the evidence they needed at his flat in Prague, and asked to be excused a moment. There was a shot from the next room; he had done what was expected of an officer and gentleman. Probably he didn't think too badly of himself in his last moments. He had no way of knowing that an Austrian archduke was about to be assassinated in Serbia, and that Europe would soon be at war. And it was only when that war began that the Austrian general staff found out just how far Redl had betrayed his country, and that the Serbians and Russians knew every detail of Austria's plans in advance. Redl was more than a traitor: he was the executioner of the Austro-Hungarian empire.

Chapter Two

THE GREAT WAR

Reginald 'Blinker' Hall

F or all practical purposes, the age of modern espionage
began on a day in September 1914, when a corpse was
dragged out of the icy waters of the Baltic clutching two
hefty books in its arms. The Russian captain of the vessel
that found him was puzzled. Why on earth should a sailor
want to leap into the sea holding heavy books, and why
hadn't he let go of them when he was drowning? The
Russian was a novice in modern warfare; it was only
September, 1914, and most naval and military men were
still naïve enough to believe that wars were fought only
with soldiers. They knew little about spies and secret codes.
His superiors in the Russian Admiralty were not much
wiser. They recognised that they had captured German
code books, handed by the captain of the sinking *Magde-
burg* to one of his men, with orders to drop them into the
sea. But it did not strike them as a particularly exciting
discovery. A few days later, the Russian attaché in London
called on Winston Churchill, and told him that they had
found the German naval code books. If the English would
care to send a ship, they were welcome to have them.

Churchill appreciated their value. He sent the ship, and
rushed the books to Admiral Oliver, head of Intelligence.
Oliver handed them to one of his best men, an ex-teacher
named Alfred Ewing. Ewing knew all about codes: he had
been trying to crack the German naval code for months.
And here it was being handed to him as a gift. It seemed too
good to be true. Either it must be some kind of a trick, or the

Germans must have already discovered their loss and changed the code. He grabbed the latest batch of coded messages, picked up from radio signals sent out from the German naval base at Wilhelmshaven. And within a few minutes, he knew that fortune had presented him with a prize. It was possible for him to read the secret orders of Grand Admiral Tirpitz and other senior commanders.

Two months later, in November 1914, Ewing was given a new boss, Captain William Reginald Hall, known as 'Blinker' (because of a twitching eyelid). The new head of Naval Intelligence did not look in the least like a spy: he was short, rotund and cheerful. In fact, he was one of the most brilliant spy-masters in the history of espionage.

The first thing Hall wanted to know was whether the codes could tell them something useful. On 14 December 1914, Ewing decoded a report that announced that the German Fleet intended to sail. Quietly, Hall moved his own ships into position in the North Sea. Two days later, Britain suffered its first naval bombardment, as ships of the German navy pounded Scarborough and Hartlepool with their heavy guns. Hall signalled his own battle cruisers, lying nearby, and told them to move in for the kill. All day, Churchill and Hall waited tensely for news. When it came, it was disappointing. Fog and rain had swept down over the North Sea as the British navy moved in. There had been a few shots exchanged, and the Germans had vanished into the mist. Churchill was disappointed. To his surprise, Hall was looking jubilant. 'There'll be a next time . . .' But that stoical reaction hardly explained his delight. He had been struck by a kind of vision. Modern warfare depended on *surprise*. The Germans had gained the element of surprise when they invaded Belgium. But ever since Marconi's discovery of radio in the 1890s, the surprise depended on a man with a transmitter and a code book. *If* he could get hold of the code books, it would be possible to anticipate every important move of the enemy. But how did one get hold of the code books? The two he had were important, but they were not the only ones.

For example, there were the strange signals coming from a transmitter in Brussels. Ewing had been working on the code for months, without success. Hall had a feeling it concealed important secrets. He ordered his spies to find out everything they could about the Brussels transmitter. This was not difficult: it had been there, in an office in the Rue de Loi, before the war. More enquiries revealed that it was operated by a young man called Alexander Szek. 'That name doesn't sound German,' said Hall thoughtfully. He made more enquiries, and suddenly knew that he was getting close to a solution. Alexander Szek, he discovered, was an Austro-Hungarian subject who had been born in Croydon, in south London, and members of his family were still living in England. Hall persuaded one of them to write Szek a letter, begging him to work for the British. A British agent in Holland smuggled it to Brussels and soon discovered that Szek was not particularly pro-German. The Germans had persuaded him to work for them because he was a good radio engineer. But he was not a born spy – the idea of stealing the German secret code terrified him. The British hinted that his family in England might be put in prison if he refused. Finally, Szek agreed.

He was not actually in possession of the code; a German Intelligence officer worked with him, and showed it to him when he needed it. But he could memorise it, a few figures at a time, and write it out. In the early months of 1915, Szek began stealing the code. Every time he completed a page, he handed it over to the British agent. But his nerve was beginning to crack. He told the agent that he wanted to be smuggled

German Foreign Secretary, Arthur Zimmerman

to England as soon as he had finished copying out the code. The agent pointed out that if he did that, the Germans would immediately change the code. But Szek was insistent. And then, one day, Szek was found dead in his room in Brussels. He appeared to have been killed by a burglar. The British later said he had been killed by the Germans. The truth, almost certainly, is that he was murdered by the British. But the Germans suddenly discovered that their 'surprise' moves were no longer surprises; their European armies found they were being outgeneralled because the enemy seemed to be able to anticipate their moves. And the day of modern espionage, the espionage of the 'cold war', had arrived.

In fact, this story, which sounds like an episode from *The Spy Who Came in From the Cold*, is grimly typical of the methods of twentieth-century spying. Blinker Hall was not a ruthless man; everyone who knew him agreed that he was cheerful, sympathetic and kindly. But he knew that if he wanted the secret codes, Szek had to be prevented from giving himself away. And since Szek was inclined to panic, there was only one answer – an 'accident'. Obviously, Hall justified the murder by saying that it saved thousands of British lives, which is true. The fact remains that it is typical of the underhand, stab-in-the-back morality of modern espionage, that appalling ruthlessness that Ian Fleming caught so well in the James Bond novels.

Blinker Hall's next triumph probably saved the Allies from losing the war.

In fact, by late 1916, they *were* losing the war. In France, the German Hindenburg Line remained unbroken, in spite of every effort the Allies made to smash through it. Britain's losses were horrific; in effect, the country was bleeding to death. Their Russian allies were also on the verge of defeat. The Germans scented victory. And since Britain depended heavily on supplies from America, the

Spies

German High Command decided to launch an all-out U-boat campaign in the Atlantic. Six months, they estimated, would be enough to bring Britain to her knees — and they were probably correct. They announced that all ships, including neutral American vessels, were liable to be sunk without warning if they were suspected of carrying supplies to the Allies.

For Germany, this move was a considerable risk. US. President Woodrow Wilson was anxious to maintain America's neutrality, but the loss of American lives might be enough to force him to enter the war. As it was, the Germans had recently shocked American opinion by accidentally sinking the British passenger liner *Lusitania*; United States sympathy was slowly turning in favour of France and Britain.

What was really needed, the Germans concluded, was a domestic war to tie-up the American army.

In November 1916, the new German Foreign Secretary, Artur Zimmermann, hit on a plan. He would contact the Mexican government and suggest an alliance against America. Germany would supply money, aid and, if America disregarded her neutrality, troops for the invasion of the southern United States. Furthermore, there was even a possibility that Japan (which was supposed to be pro-Ally) might be persuaded into helping the invasion. For years they had been treated as a minor power by the Americans; approached tactfully, they might well throw their weight behind Germany.

The plan may strike a modern reader as absurd, but in 1916 it stood a good chance of success. The Mexicans, smarting at decades of indignities inflicted on them by their powerful neighbour, knew that if they successfully conquered one or two of the southern states — say Arizona and New Mexico — they might go on to become the most powerful nation in the Americas. At the time the United States Army was far from full mobilisation. With the support of the Germans – and possibly the Japanese – Mexico stood a good fighting chance in a lightning war.

There was a problem; Zimmermann had no direct method of contacting his agents in Mexico and time was of the essence. In desperation he decided on a considerable gamble. President Wilson had set-up a telegraph hot-line in the White House to facilitate peace negotiations with the Germans. On 16 January, 1917, Zimmermann simply sent his coded message to the White House with an uncoded request to pass it on to the German Embassy. Provided the Americans did not know how to unscramble the code, they would do as they were asked as a matter of courtesy. The embassy could then wire the coded part of the message to Mexico via the public, Western Union telegraph.

What Zimmerman did not know was that Blinker Hall's men were tapping the German-White House hot-line, and that they knew how to break German codes. It was unfortunate that, due to the large backlog of diplomatic trivia that had accumulated from the hot-line, it was not until just before 1 February, 1917 – the day Germany declared unrestricted U-boat war – that Blinker Hall's cipher department started to decode Zimmermann's message.

President Wilson – a man who felt all wars were wasteful and barbaric – had decided to turn the other cheek when the Germans threatened to sink American shipping. Against a growing force of public opinion, he insisted on the US remaining a neutral peace-maker. Even the fact that the Allies were losing the war failed to move him. This is why Blinker Hall, long infuriated by what he saw as American dithering, read the Zimmermann document with a chortle of satisfaction, then called Edward Bell, a friend in the American embassy in London, and read him the message.

President Woodrow Wilson

Although now almost extinct, covert anarchist organisations were at the top of Scotland Yard's list of threats to the state at the turn of the century. On the continent, the anti-authoritarians had murdered the French President, the Russian Tsar and numerous officials. In Britain they bombed three post offices, a Mayfair shop and an underground train, and shot several policemen. As spiritual forerunners of the communist Red Brigades, anarchist clubs lived in secret communes – robbing to get money and discussing political philosophy over home-made bombs.

The end of their activities in Britain was signalled by the famous Sidney Street Siege in January, 1911. Anarchist hero, Peter the Painter and his gang were tracked by police to their east London safehouse. After a five hour gun battle the building caught fire and was soon a blazing ruin. Two of the gang were found dead inside, but Peter the Painter apparently escaped.

Later researchers have suggested that the mysterious Peter was not an anarchist at all, but actually an member of the Russian Ochrana Secret Police, sent to London to act as an agent provocateur. Whatever the case, Peter the Painter disappeared from the anarchist scene following the siege.

Bell's first reaction was profound mistrust – he felt it had it had British plot written all over it. Blinker Hall countered that all they had to do to confirm the message was check the records at the White House and Western Union. Bell did just this, and realised that this left no doubt of the telegram's authenticity. It meant that the Germans were conspiring against the security of the USA, which was an act of war.

In the White House, President Wilson studied the communication with incredulity and shock. Upon reading the following line he is said to have come close to fainting:

'WE MAKE MEXICO A PROPOSAL OF ALLIANCE ON THE FOLLOWING BASIS: MAKE WAR TOGETHER MAKE PEACE TOGETHER GENEROUS FINANCIAL SUPPORT AND AN UNDERSTANDING ON OUR PART THAT MEXICO IS TO RECOVER THE LOST TERRITORY IN TEXAS NEW MEXICO AND ARIZONA. THE SETTLEMENT IN DETAIL IS LEFT TO YOU.'

The pro-war party in the US government made sure the Zimmermann message was leaked to the press and, while the public was reeling from the revelation, news came that three American ships had been sunk without warning by German U-boats. Even the pacifists in Wilson's cabinet told the shattered president that he must declare war on Germany. This happened on 6 April, 1917. As vast numbers of American troops and supplies poured across the Atlantic – too many to be stopped by the U-boats – Blinker Hall had good reason to feel deeply pleased with himself. He had tipped the balance of the war in favour of the Allies. The American forces played a vital part in breaking the deadlock in France, and just over a year later, on 9 November, 1918, the abdication of Kaiser Wilhelm II was announced in Berlin. Two days later, on 11 November, Germany surrendered.

Mata Hari

Although she is perhaps the single most famous female spy in history, Gerda Zelle — better known as Mata Hari — never regarded herself as a genuine secret agent. Neither, it seems, did the men who eventually convicted her of espionage.

Margaretha Gertruidia Zelle was born on 7 August, 1876, in Leeuwarden, Holland. Her background was solidly bourgeois; her father was a hatter, and both parents came from respectable, middle-class Dutch families.

Although not conventionally beautiful — even when young — Gerda had olive skin, Oriental features, almond eyes and an indefinable sexual allure. At fourteen she could pass for seventeen, and did so whenever she could. When she attended a teacher's training college, the principal became so noticeably infatuated with her she had to be hurriedly withdrawn. A year later, when she was eighteen and living under the close supervision of an aunt in the Hague, Gerda managed to meet her future husband through a newspaper lonely hearts column. Captain Rudolf MacLeod, a Dutch officer of Scottish descent, was 39 years old and a confirmed bachelor. He had just returned from a posting in the Dutch East Indies and was regularly teased by his friends for not being married. One of these, without MacLeod's knowledge, posted the advertisement as a practical joke, and the irritated officer had received and thrown away fourteen replies before he came to Gerda's. Her passionate and sexually explicit letter intrigued him. They met and swiftly became lovers; not long after this, she discovered she was pregnant, and — in spite of determined opposition from his upper-class family — were married. Gerda would later represent him as a drunken cad, yet his decision to stand by her — when he might easily have had himself posted back to Java — speaks in his favour.

Unfortunately, Gerda showed very little inclination to motherhood, neglecting their son Norman and disappearing for hours at a time. When questioned, she refused to say where she had been. Fearing she was having an affair, Macleod was relieved to be promoted to major and posted to command a reserve battalion in Java. Once they were out there, however, her behaviour only became worse.

There can be little doubt that Gerda's enthusiasm for men bordered on nymphomania. Finding herself the first lady of a garrison town, she made herself unpopular by snubbing the officers' wives and bedding their husbands. Major MacLeod, when not engaged on regimental business, seems to have collapsed into alcoholism and melancholia. In later years, Gerda claimed that his debauches drove her to other men, and that he frequently returned home from another woman's bed to beat and drag her about the house by her hair.

Gerda gave birth to a daughter in 1898, but this does not seem to have healed the rift. Their son died the following year, and when MacLeod caught Gerda in bed with one of his junior officers, he decided to return to Holland, where they separated. Macleod retained custody of their daughter.

Gerda now found herself in dire financial straits. Her husband made a small allowance, but had disowned her numerous debts – her love of luxury was another lifelong characteristic.

At 27 she moved to Paris, she became an artist's model, then a prostitute. At this low-point of her career, she was spotted by a talent scout and recruited to one of Paris' many high-class brothels. There she learned, or rather refined, her skills as a courtesan.

When in Java she had watched the dances of the native girls with fascination, and had devised a few of her own. Paris at the turn of the century, enjoying a reputation for decadence, was in the grip of a fashion for all things exotic and Oriental. Gerda listened to the applause and realised she had a valuable skill after all.

Calling herself Lady Gresha MacLeod (possibly to defy her stuffy in-laws) she entertained at private parties by performing her pseudo-Oriental dances on the dinner table. To further emphasise the litheness of her movements she performed naked. Of course, strippers were two-a-penny in Paris at the time, but Gerda's sinuous sexuality set her apart from the other bachelor party girls. A well-known personality in the Paris theatrical world took her under his wing and into his bed, and on his advice, Gerda created a whole new persona for herself. She was no longer Gerda MacLeod – Dutch hatter's daughter and ex-officer's wife – but mysterious Mata Hari; temple dancer and Indian princess.

She told her admirers, in lilting French with an eastern accent, that she was born in southern India, the child of a high-caste Brahmin priest and a *bajadere* – a holy temple dancer. Her mother, only fourteen, had died bearing her, and she, as tradition dictated, had been trained to follow in her footsteps. The priests had named her Mata Hari – meaning Eye of the Morning. In her thirteenth year she had been ritually deflowered, then danced the holy dance, naked on the temple alter. Later she had been lured away by a British officer who had fallen in love with her from afar. They had married and she had borne him a son. This boy had been poisoned by a jealous servant and the officer, stricken with grief, had died of fever. (The murder of the child might have been the only true element in her story – it is possible that young Norman MacLeod was poisoned by a Javanese maid because Major MacLeod had beaten her husband). Left unprotected from the vengeful priests of her sect, she had fled to Europe and now made a meagre living displaying her dancing skills to discerning clients.

Never one to waste time on trivial details, her story was full of holes – even the name Mata Hari is Javanese, not Hindi – but nobody was unkind enough to question its contradictions. Mata Hari was an alluring mystery, and her new act featured Oriental silks, burnt spices, and a venerable greybeard who explained the holy legends represented by each dance. Her performance was now considered art rather than striptease, and she presented it to mixed audiences in the grandest locations. All Paris talked about her, and fashionable parties were considered incomplete without her presence. She swiftly became a turn-of-the-century super-star.

She was now able to indulge her passion for the opposite sex with the cream of society. For young officers and clubmen, it became something of a status symbol to say you had spent the night with Mata Hari, and more than one Crown Prince is said to have gone to Paris with expressly that purpose. When Rudolf MacLeod finally divorced her in 1906, the case went uncontested.

By this time, to her disgust, several other ladies of equal gifts had set-up in the Oriental dancing game, and she complained that these imitations 'degraded nude dancing'. But, noting that her rivals were all younger than she was – she decided it was time to move on. In 1907 she left Paris for Berlin.

Her instinct was sound; the Berliners received her with even more enthusiasm than the French. Parisians enjoy the subtle emotions associated with *l'amour*; Berliners have always enjoyed cruder forms of eroticism, and Mata Hari's dancing came close to visual pornography. Crown Prince Wilhelm is alleged to have been one of her conquests, and when he took her with him on army manoeuvres in Silesia, she is reported to have danced naked on the generals' mess table.

By 1914 she was thirty-seven, and a life of passion had left its marks on her face. It was probably soon thereafter that she was approached by German Secret Service with the proposal that she should spy for Germany — although some biographers claim she was sent to a spy-school near Basel as early as 1910. It seems likely that she was housed in a luxury apartment, and introduced to men of high rank from other nations, passing on anything she learned to her spy-masters. What is certain is that in July, 1914, three nights before the outbreak of the Great War, she was observed by a member of the British Secret Service meeting with the Police President of Berlin, a man called von Jagow, and money was seen to change hands over the dinner table. The post of Police President included control of the Prussian secret police (later to become the Gestapo). At her later trial, since there was no way to pass off such a meeting as innocent, Mata Hari admitted to being paid 30,000 marks by von Jagow — but insisted the money had been a long-overdue payment for entertaining guests of the German government. A likelier explanation is that von Jagow was giving her severance pay. Now Germany was about to go to war, her role as a seducer of foreign soldiers and diplomats was redundant.

Following her meeting with von Jagow, Mata Hari returned to her hotel in seemingly genuine distress. There she met a Dutch businessman, to whom she represented herself as a Russian dancer who was trapped by the war. He sent her to Holland to stay in his house in Amsterdam. On his return, Mata Hari contrived to have an affair with him under the same roof as his wife. But when she revealed that she was, in fact, as Dutch as he was and that her ex-husband was living only a few streets away, he decided to end the affair.

Holland remained neutral for the entire war, and became an international centre of espionage activity. As far as we know, Mata Hari was not involved. For the next year she seems to have lived quietly in Amsterdam, living off what lovers she could. A half-hearted attempt to revive her dancing career proved a disastrous failure and the show closed on the first night. Then, in the summer of 1915, she travelled to Paris once again. Many claims have been made concerning what Mata Hari's accomplishments were in the field of espionage. It has been said that she was the Head of the German secret service in France. That, disguised as a Red Cross nurse and attending a wounded Russian officer she described passionately as 'the only man I ever loved', she stole top secret French defence plans, including the all important defences at Verdun. She has been personally credited with the betrayal of 66 French agents operating in Germany and, indirectly, the sinking of 17 British troop transports. One of her lovers in the French High Command supposedly let her see details of the crucial defence Plan XVII. Another beau, this time a British officer, is said to have told her all about the Allies' new secret weapon known as the tank. She has even been accused of being responsible for the death Field-Marshal Lord Kitchener, by stealing British naval plans that allowed the Germans to sink his cruiser off the Orkneys. All of the above, and most of the other espionage feats attributed to Mata Hari have been proved untrue. In fact, it is very possible she provided the Germans with little or no useful information during her whole career as a spy.

Mata Hari's own explanation of why she went to Paris was that she was short of money and wanted to sell some of expensive possessions she had left in France when she went to Germany. There seems no reason to disbelieve this story, although it was certainly not the whole truth. While in Paris, she wrote many letters to a certain German major in Amsterdam, via the Dutch diplomatic bag. In return the officer sent her letters and money. It may be, as Mata Hari later claimed, that he was only a lover from her Berlin days, with whom she had become re-acquainted in Amsterdam. The fact was, however, the major just happened .to be the Head of German espionage activities in Holland.

It took only a few weeks to sell her assets in France, but Mata Hari stayed on for seven months. During this time she visited the eastern front, but does not appear to have been in a position to hear anything other than common gossip among the troops. On her return she unexpectedly offered to spy for the French Secret Service.

The Deuxieme Bureau, as it was known, had been officially aware of Mata Hari's existence for some time. In fact, they had been keeping an eye on her since the beginning of the year. The British had quite specifically warned them not to employ her after the von Jagow incident, and their own investigations indicated that she had been employed by the Germans before the war. However, her offer was deeply tempting to the French. As a espionage weapon for either side, Mata Hari had considerable potential. Her list of international contacts was enormous, as was her list of ex-lovers among Germany's junker class. The blackmail angle alone was staggering. The only question was whether she genuinely wanted to work for France, or was a double-agent for Germany.

To test her trustworthiness, they pretended to accept, and asked her if she was willing to undertake a mission into German-occupied Belgium. She was given a list of six contacts and told to wait for further instructions. In fact, the mission was a trap. Five of the contacts were known double-agents — criminals released from jail by the Germans on condition they offered their services as Allied spies. The sixth man, however, was a genuine agent. If Mata Hari betrayed the names, the sixth man would be arrested by the Germans. Shortly after her arrival in Belgium, news came that the agent had been

Mata Hari

captured and shot. This, the Deuxieme Bureau concluded, proved Mata Hari's duplicity.

But this was thrown into doubt by a communication from the British Secret Service. The executed agent had apparently been *their* man all along. They had planted him to infiltrate the German Secret Service, and his work for the French had simply been a sideline to collect two sets of wages. Furthermore, the British had proof that the agent had been betrayed from Paris. So it looked, after all, as if she was innocent. Undecided, the Deuxieme Bureau waited for her to report-in, but she never did.

The next definite sighting was in mid-1916, in Madrid. French agents in Spain kept Mata Hari under surveillance, but made no effort to contact her. She seems to have been aware she was under observation and, at one point recognising the agent tailing her, stopped to have a chat. She openly told him that she was in contact with a German bank in Madrid and the German consulate in Vigo, implying she was spying on them. The Deuxieme Bureau, however, still received no reports from her.

In November, 1916, Mata Hari boarded the *Hollandia*, bound for Rotterdam. On passing into the English Channel, the ship was halted by a cruiser of the British blockade, and ordered to put into Falmouth. Officers from Scotland Yard were waiting for Mata Hari on the dockside. It emerged that British agents had also been watching her in Spain, and that when she set sail the British decided to find-out, once and for all, whose side she was on.

In London, she was interviewed by Assistant Commissioner, Sir Basil Thomson, the head of Special Branch. Sir Basil reported that he was surprised by Mata Hari's appearance. He had expected, or perhaps hoped to see, the glamorous temptress of the stories — Delilah in the flesh, so to speak. Instead he was confronted by a tall, dignified, middle-aged lady of aristocratic manners, still beautiful and highly self-possessed.

Sir Basil challenged her over her German friends in Madrid; far from denying them she added to his list of names. She had, she said, many friends of many nationalities; as a neutral Dutch subject she had every right to associate with whom she pleased. As the questioning went on, however, Mata Hari plainly realised where Sir Basil was leading her. She surprised him by suddenly laughing and saying; 'You are quite wrong. I am a spy, but not for the Germans. I'm a French spy.'

Sir Basil was completely taken aback by this revelation, and promptly wired the French to find if it was true. What they replied is not certain, but it must have been favourable, since Sir Basil then decided to release her. Yet there can be no doubt that they must have been embarrassed to admit that she was supposed to be in their employ. Several writers have suggested that Mata Hari signed her own death warrant by invoking French protection.

The British were plainly unhappy at the turn of events, but had to let Mata Hari go. Nevertheless, they had no intention of letting her return to Holland. Instead, she was placed on a boat back to Spain. As they parted, Sir Basil, dropped his official tone, and said: 'Madame, if you will accept the advise of one nearly twice your age, give up what you have been doing.'

On her arrival back in Madrid Mata Hari seems to have laid her problems at the door of the German authorities. What exactly did she think she was doing? The answer is probably that she simply wanted to keep body and soul together. Her career as a dancer was over; she had no current husband or lover to support her. The French were unlikely to pay her. That left only the Germans. The embassy telegraphed to their Intelligence HQ in Amsterdam saying:

'Agent H.21 in Madrid. Has got herself into French Service but taken off by British cruiser and sent back; demands instructions and money.'

A reply duly came back. In fact, the French had cracked the particular cipher, and decoded both messages. Years later, the head of the Deuxieme Bureau cipher department published what he claimed was the second telegram transcript. It said:

'Good pre-war agent. We have given her nothing since the war. Let her have 15,000 francs.'

In other words, the Germans were exposing Mata Hari as a spy by admitting that she had been a pre-war agent, yet also stating that she had not been working for them during the war.

Mata Hari now made her final mistake. Instead of taking the money and lying low until the war was over, she walked straight back into the lion's mouth. When she was picked-up shortly after visiting the Dutch embassy in Paris, she still had the German cheque in her handbag. It was practically an admission of guilt. She was brought before a court-martial on 24 July, 1917, and the trial was held in camera. It lasted two days, but the outcome was certain before it began.

In her defence, she insisted that the many payments from Germany over the years were gifts from lovers. The letters she had sent via the Dutch diplomatic bag she claimed were to her daughter and her lover in Amsterdam. Of her numerous contacts and lovers in German high society and the High Command, she replied; 'I am not French, so what is to prevent my having friends of any nationality I choose?'

It is clear that she failed to grasp the seriousness of the situation. She was aware that she might be executed as a spy, but probably thought the idea absurd. She had not done any spying for years, and even then, it had been amateur stuff, persuading foreign diplomats to tell her their secrets as they lay beside her after lovemaking. She probably saw it all as a game.

The French took a less casual attitude. She had joined their secret service, then failed to report in. And she had

It is now generally accepted that Mata Hari was, at best, an ineffective spy. Banda on the other hand – the woman believed by some to have been Mata Hari's illegitimate daughter – had a spectacular espionage career.

Born in Java – where Mata Hari spent her tempestuous married years – Banda was said to have been a Eurasian beauty with a sharp intellect. When her Dutch lover died in 1935, she inherited his wealth and was soon considered a leading social figure in Batavia. Her spying career began when the Japanese invaded in 1941, and forced her to collect information for them. What they did not suspect was that she was giving them useless information while feeding their secrets to the Allies. Following the war, when the Dutch tried to reclaim the colony, she stole their military plans, turning the tide in the favour of the Indonesian nationalists. Following the Communist revolution in China, the Americans employed her to infiltrate the Chinese Red Army.

Sadly, her luck ran out in 1950, when she was sent to North Korea to report on the coming invasion of the South. A fellow Indonesian, who had worked under her during the war and now worked for the Chinese, recognised and denounced her. Like her reputed mother, she was sent to face a firing squad.

escaped internment in Britain describing herself as a French spy. Whatever else she was, she was certainly an intolerable embarrassment.

It was when being questioned about her offer to spy for the French that she began to flounder.

'I told the French authorities many places in Morocco where German U-boats call to refuel. It was very useful information, I am told.'

No doubt, replied the prosecutor grimly, but how, if she was only a dancer as she said, did she become a party to such detailed military information? Caught off guard, Mata Hari began a rambling explanation that she was plainly making-up as she when along. Eventually she broke off, perhaps realising how ridiculous her story sounded.

The question of her espionage number, H.21, which had been mentioned in the first telegram, was also raised by the prosecution. Surely, they said, this proved beyond all doubt that she was a German spy? The defence countered by showing that the prefix 'H' was known to indicate agents recruited before the war. In conjunction with the second telegram, this evidence might have been enough to save Mata Hari's life – if the French had any intention of sparing it.

It is still not clear why the court decided to sentence her to death. Could it have been that if she had simply been interned – as most later experts considered the appropriate sentence – she would have been free to continue a vendetta of embarrassing revelations against them on her release? Certainly, every French official who had ever slept with her had good reason to want to see her silenced. Whatever the reason, and in the face of the evidence, the court decided to find her guilty, and she was sentenced to death by firing squad.

She showed remarkable courage up to the moment the sentence was carried out on 15 October, 1917, even refusing a blindfold.

Her subsequent elevation to the role of the world's greatest female spy certainly has no basis in fact. The truth seems to be that Mata Hari never acted as a spy in wartime. But in any case, she lacked the temperament for espionage – she was essentially a scatterbrained nymphomaniac who had little thought to spare for anything but her present – and her next – lover. Only the legend of Mata Hari the *femme fatale* seems to explain why the French have continued to insist that her execution was justified.

Chapter Three

WORLD WAR II

The most devastating conflict in human history was also the first in which the final outcome was decisively influenced by the use, and misuse, of spies.

Richard Sorge

It is generally agreed that Sorge was probably the greatest spy of all time. Born in Russia in 1895, Sorge's family moved to Germany when he was a child. As a student he became passionately left-wing; he joined the German Communist Party, and eventually became its intelligence chief. He trained in Russia, then moved around Europe, building up spy-rings in Scandivania and England. (The British Secret Service spotted him fairly quickly; after that, Sorge always maintained that it was one of the best in the world.) In Russia in the late twenties, he was involved in clashes between the Army Secret Service and the Secret Police (K.G.B.), and his fate might well have been the same as that of Yagoda; fortunately, the Communists decided that he would be useful in the Far East. And this was the sphere of the sensational operations that have made him the most famous name in espionage. His instructions were simple. The Soviets were already convinced that the great threats of the future would come from Germany and Japan; Sorge's job was to set up a spy network in Japan.

He was well qualified for the job. A highly intelligent man, who spoke several languages, he also had the perfect cover. He was an ardent womaniser. His success with beautiful women was phenomenal. (It is interesting that many of the great spies have been womanisers – Wollweber was another – as if spying and love affairs were complementary activities.) With so many shreds of scandal attached to his name, and a reputation for being an incorrigible philanderer, who could believe that Sorge was also a spy and a top level communist official? He didn't seem to be serious enough.

In Japan, Sorge began to recruit colleagues: Agnes Smedley, a well-known author of books on China, and a friend of Mao Tse Tung; Ozaki, a Japanese correspondent; a Yugoslav pressman, Voukelitch. Slowly, Sorge built up an intelligence network in China. Then, when Hitler came to power in 1933, he was given another task: to spy on the Germans in Japan. There was one important preliminary: Sorge applied for membership of the Nazi Party. And Hitler's Intelligence system was so poor that Sorge was given a party card. Back in Japan, Sorge completed his own Japanese spy network with the addition of an American-Japanese, Miyagi Yotuka. Miyagi and Ozaki were ordered to form their own network of Japanese spies.

Sorge's charm soon made him a favoured guest at the German Embassy. He became friendly with an assistant military attaché, Lieutenant Colonel Eugen Ott. No one ever suspected that the philandering correspondent of the *Frankfurt Times* was a Russian spy. Ozaki became a leading member of a 'breakfast club' of Japanese intellectuals, with close connections with the cabinet. It was he who told Sorge in advance of Japan's projected attack on China: information that delighted the Kremlin, because while Japan was fighting China, it was unlikely to invade Russia. And when Colonel Ott was appointed German ambassador, Sorge then had sources of information about German and Japanese policies that made him the most important secret agent in the world. Sorge knew about the Japanese attack on Pearl Harbour weeks before it happened. He knew the exact date when the Germans intended to invade Russia, and if it had not been for Stalin's stupidity in ignoring his information — convinced that Hitler was a man of his word — Operation Barbarossa would have been defeated within days.

The head of Japanese Intelligence, Colonel Osaki (not to be confused with the spy Ozaki) knew there was a major spy network in Japan: his radio receivers picked up their coded messages, but he could not read them. Finally, he became convinced that Sorge was his man. He knew Sorge's great weakness — women. (At one point, Sorge had even risked breaking up the network by having an affair with Voukelitch's mistress.) He asked a German attaché to arrange a meeting with Sorge at a nightclub. Over a bottle of *saké*, he told Sorge about the beautiful girl who danced in the cabaret — about how many men were in love with her. Sorge was curious and his curiosity was increased by the mask the girl wore. He began to spend every evening at the cabaret, until finally the girl became his mistress. But she was an agent of Colonel Osaki — an aristocratic Japanese girl who had been asked to sacrifice herself for her country.

One night Sorge stopped his car and started to make love to the girl; he wanted her to come back and spend the night with him, because he felt his work in Japan was completed at last. He took out his cigarette case and a tiny roll of paper fell out. Sorge carefully tore it up and threw it out of the car window. The girl made an excuse to get to a telephone and rang Japanese Intelligence; almost as soon as the car drove away, Japanese agents were collecting the torn fragments of paper. The next morning, as Sorge lay asleep beside the girl, Colonel Osaki walked into the bedroom. He handed Sorge a piece of paper — the message he thought he had destroyed. Sorge stood up and bowed. He knew he was defeated.

According to one account, Sorge faced his executioners, in November 1944, with complete nonchalance, smoking a cigarette. But there is no definite evidence that Sorge *was* executed. We know that he claimed a reprieve on the grounds that he was a Soviet citizen, and that Russia was not at war with Japan. A British diplomat who knew Sorge claimed that he saw him in Shanghai in 1947. And it was at about this time that the girl who had betrayed Sorge was murdered. It seems possible that he ended his days behind a desk in the G.R.U. headquarters in Moscow.

Cicero

The Japanese were not alone in having their top secrets stolen and delivered direct to the enemy. Throughout 1943 and 1944 an Axis spy in the British Embassy in Ankara photographed all kinds of classified information, including details of the Casablanca conference, the British diplomatic code, the names of most of the British spies in Turkey, and the date and location of the D-day landings. Yet the agent Elyesa Bazna – code named Cicero – only took-up spying because he had failed at everything else.

At 38, Bazna – a short, thick-set Turk – had been a locksmith, taxi driver, fireman, concert singer and burglar, and failed in every one of them. In 1943, as a last resort, he decided to try his hand at espionage. He had been chauffeur and valet to Albert Jenke, First Secretary at the German embassy in Turkey (who was also the brother in law of Ribbentropp, the German foreign minister). Jenke had dismissed him for practising his hobby – photography – on his personal correspondence. Banza later admitted that he had merely allowed his curiosity to get the better of him, but that when he came to think about it later, it struck him that his hobby might, after all, be turned to commercial advantage. All he needed was the right job and a less observant employer.

In 1943, the French Resistance made a major attempt to reorganise their operations against the occupying Germans. They had been largely under the control of the Special Operations Executive (S.O.E.) in London, but now, as a matter of national pride, the French wanted to run their own show. Unfortunately, the efforts of their nominal leader, Jean Moulin, were hampered by his constant wrangling with his subordinates. The S.O.E. liaison man was also horrified by the French lack of security consciousness: Moulin often conducted screaming rows over Resistance policy in his thin-walled Paris flat, where anyone might overhear.

Disaster struck in June of that year when Moulin and the members of the National Council of the Resistance attended a secret meeting near Lyons. They were surprised by the Gestapo and captured to a man. The situation was made worse by the fact that Moulin, who hated to delegate responsibility, had burdened himself with more information about the Resistance than anyone else in France. The Germans had in their hands the power to totally annihilate the French Secret Army, but Moulin, despite his other failings, proved to be a heroically brave man. The Gestapo thugs tortured and eventually beat him to death, but he told them nothing.

His decision to try the British embassy was made at random. He declared frankly that he felt allegiance only to money, and that the outcome of the war, in which Turkey

Elyesa Bazna, code name 'Cicero'

was not involved, was a matter of total indifference to him.

One day, loitering in the lobby of the Ankara Palace Hotel, he happened to see a newspaper advertisement for a valet inserted by Douglas Busk, the British First Secretary. He applied for the job immediately, and was accepted.

As things turned-out, Bazna had reason to believe his luck had finally taken a turn for the better. In spite of his previous service at the German embassy, no óne seems to have considered that he might be a security risk. He was delighted to find that the job was ideal for a novice spy to learn his trade: his new employer was in the habit of bringing his work home with him, and often left secret files lying about the suite. Bazna dutifully tidied these up, and then studied and photographed them.

Unfortunately, none of the secrets Busk carelessly allowed his servant to copy were particularly saleable. The most highly classified document he managed to steal contained details of Winston Churchill's attempt to pressure Turkey to enter the war on the side of the Allies. But the Germans could have guessed as much anyway, since they were doing the same thing. They would be unlikely to pay much to have the obvious confirmed, and Bazna did not dare approach them unless he knew that he had something worth the risk.

Bazna began to fear that his promising new career would founder like the others. Then the British Ambassador himself, Sir Hughe Knatchbull-Hugessen, announced he was in need of a valet. Bazna pulled strings to get the job. To be more be precise, he seduced the nursemaid to the Busk family. She argued his case to Mrs Busk and she, in turn, put pressure on her husband. The First Secretary seems to have been glad to recommend his valet for a technical promotion and Sir Hughe accepted his suggestion. Bazna was thus able to secure the post without the tiresome formality of an interview (which would have included a security check).

Spies

Bazna was understandably worried that Sir Hughe would be more security-minded than the First Secretary, but his mind was soon set at rest. If anything, the ambassador was even more careless. Shortly after arriving, the valet was able to make wax impressions of his master's keys while Sir Hughe was taking his morning bath – keys that were never supposed to be out of the ambassador's sight. Bazna was then able to open the high security diplomatic red boxes, but he soon found that this was scarcely necessary; the ambassador was in the habit of taking top secret documents to bed with him and reading himself to sleep. The apprentice spy once again, found he could combine espionage with housework.

Now he had a few top-class diplomatic secrets, Bazna finally felt ready to approach his old employer, the German First Secretary. Jenke, remembering their previous 'misunderstanding', was inclined to suspect Bazna was a British double agent, but, nevertheless introduced the valet to his intelligence attache, a man called Moyzisch. Bazna presented him with photographic films of more that fifty British top secret documents and told him the price was £20,000. Moyzisch was shocked at the enormous sum, and said that the embassy simply did not have that kind of money. In that case, said Bazna, he could offer them to the Soviet embassy, which was just around the corner. But why did Moyzisch not get the photographs developed, and then make up his mind?

When Moyzisch saw the photographs, he knew he had an incredible bargain. He handed over the £20,000 in sterling, and told the valet that he would buy all the documents he could provide at the same rate. Bazna, who refused to give his name (Jenke claimed, untruthfully, that it had been six years since he had employed him, and had forgotten his name), was given the code name Cicero. He was also given a Leica camera and as much film as he could use – since buying film would obviously place him at risk. Bazna/Cicero returned jubilantly to his apartment at the British Embassy and hid the money beneath the carpet. If his luck held he was going to be a very rich man . . .

Over the next few months, Bazna provided the Germans with hundreds of documents – in fact he rather overdid it, for the German ambassador, on the strength of a Cicero document, accused the Turks of violating their neutrality by allowing British military personnel to entry the country disguised as civilians. This led to an immediate security check at the British Embassy. Staff with access to confidential papers were thoroughly grilled, door and window locks were changed, and intrusion warning systems were fitted. But the ambassador's valet was not interviewed since he had no official access to diplomatic documents. He could come and go as he pleased and his staff bedroom, with a growing fortune beneath the carpet, was never searched.

Cicero's eventual unmasking was the work of two other secret agents. The first was a spy the Americans had planted in the Nazi Foreign Ministry in Berlin. This agent reported a prodigiously productive agent in the British embassy in Ankara, but could only offer the code name Cicero as identification. Unlike the Germans, the Americans had no illusions whatever about British security – even at that stage of the war, British incompetence had cost them heavily. Consequently, they decided not to inform their ally of the danger, but instead, to plant their own agent in the German embassy in Ankara to discover Cicero's true name and position. It was felt that any British involvement might lead to a greater muddle.

The American plant was the daughter of a German diplomat, Cornelia Knapp. An attractive twenty-three-year-old, she had lived most of her life in America, and her sympathies were entirely with the Allies. She applied to become secretary to Intelligence Attache Moyzisch and was immediately accepted. Her father's good standing, and the fact that her brothers were fighting in the German armed forces, served as an effective cover.

She soon discovered that her task was far from straightforward. Moyzisch himself did not know Cicero's name – all the documents referred to him by his code name alone. As time passed, Cornelia began to feel signs of nervous strain. As a German citizen, she could expect a grim fate at the hands of the Gestapo if she were caught going through her employer's top secret files. On the other hand, she had to grab every opportunity to search Moyzisch's papers on the offchance of spotting some minuscule clue to the identity of Cicero.

Moyzisch noted his secretary's tension and thoughtfully suggested that she take a trip back to Germany to visit her parents over Easter. This, of course, only increased the pressure on Cornelia Knapp.

Fortunately, she once came into contact with Bazna, and a little sleuthing finally revealed that the spy was the British ambassador's valet. The discovery came only just in time. Moyzisch was waiting at the station to put her on a train to Berlin when she passed on the vital piece of information to the American Secret Service, and was flown to Cairo to be debriefed. She received no payment for her work, but the Americans granted her the right to something she valued more than money – the right to live in America. She returned there and settled in California with an American husband.

Moyzisch, after his fruitless wait at the station, began to suspect the truth. He contacted Cicero and told him to get out. Bazna packed his bags and, with a certain panache, presented his resignation before escaping. He carried with him £300,000 from under the carpet.

What Bazna stole for the Nazis was worth every penny of the money. He gave them the power to eliminate or neutralise almost all the British agents in Turkey, translate British diplomatic codes, and ambush and slaughter the Allies in their D-Day offensive. Fortunately, the Nazis failed to make use of any of these opportunities. For although the German embassy had no doubt of the value of Cicero's information, the High Command though otherwise. Ribbentrop, the Nazi Foreign Minister, could not be convinced that Cicero was not a British plant. No spy, he insisted, could have regular access to that sort of information. He appeared to accept the Cicero documents as part of a double-bluff to confuse the Allies. Anything received from the Ankara embassy was filed under 'disinformation' and forgotten.

Moyzisch himself came under suspicion, and was ordered to return to Germany. He delayed implementing the order until the Turks entered the war on the side of the Allies, when he cheerfully accepted internment for the rest of the war.

The only winner, it might seem, was Elyesa Bazna. But Bazna learned too late that Ribbentropp had regarded him as a British agent, and paid him in counterfeit cash. His carefully hoarded cache of £5 notes was worthless. Earlier in the war the Nazis, in an attempt to destabilise the British economy, had forged millions of £5 notes. The plan had failed because there was no practical way to secretly introduce that much money into the world banking system – and when a few cash-crammed containers were experimentally dropped over Britain, people simply handed them in at the local police stations. Cicero had been paid off in worthless paper – as he discoverd when he tried to set up in business. The bank of England swiftly rejected the forgeries, and although Bazna succeeded in convincing the Turks that he was the victim of a Nazi swindle, he found himself no better off than before. He tried suing the new German government in Bonn, but they declined to accept responsibilty for the Nazi swindle. Cicero was made to pay back tradesmen whom he had paid with the fake money.

Yet both he and Moyzisch eventually made a profit. Moyzisch published a book about Cicero, *Operation Cicero* which sold well. The British public were inclined to be incredulous until Mr Ernest Bevin was forced to admit in Parliament that it was all true. Cicero himself went on to write *I Was Cicero*, which was made into a film with James Mason playing the leading role. So Bazna was not entirely mistaken when he believed that his luck had taken a turn for the better when he became the British ambassador's valet.

Operation Mincemeat

One of the most brilliant espionage operations of the Second World War was also one of the most macabre. British Intelligence, generally regarded of as one of the more gentlemanly spying organisations, devised a plan so extreme that their German counterparts were caught completely off guard. The ironically named Operation Mincemeat was a complete success, largely because the Nazis could not believe the Allies were capable of such ghoulish behaviour.

Following their final victory on the North African Front in 1943, the Allies faced a major problem. Winston Churchill had made it a personal crusade that the next major Anglo-American offensive should be in Italy: the 'soft under-belly of Europe', as he called it. Allied planners insisted that a direct assault on Southern Italy was too dangerous. The island of Sicily would need to be captured first to provide a base of operations, but even this was a risky venture. Allied Intelligence was also reasonably sure that Vichy French spies in the captured French colonies of North Africa would be sending news of any Allied military build-up to the Nazis. If Mussolini guessed their intentions, he would fortify the rocky island and reinforce the garrison, and any attempted landing might well turn into a massacre.

That is, unless Mussolini could be tricked into believing the blow was to fall elsewhere.

The idea for Mincemeat was the brainchild of a Royal Navy Lieutenant Commander named Ewan Montagu, who may have been inspired by the World War One story of the corpse that was pulled out of the Baltic clutching the German code books. Montagu's suggestion was that papers about a fictitious Allied offensive could be left on the dead body of a staff officer, in a place where the enemy were bound to find him.

The plan presented major problems from the outset. The war, of course, provided an endless supply of spare corpses, but the decoy would have to be convincing enough to survive a post mortem by skilled pathologists. Then there was the problem of getting the scheme accepted – what if the various problems were overcome, then the plan had to be dropped due to the moral outrage of some a general or leading politician.

At least that problem was soon solved. When the plan was submitted to Churchill and Eisenhower, both gave it their full support.

It was decided that the body was to be washed up on a Spanish beach, dressed in the uniform of a major in the Royal Marines. Chained to its wrist would be a locked diplomatic case and inside this would be a letter – supposedly from Lord Mountbatten to General Alexander in Africa, which would contain references to preparations for an invasion of Sardinia with a diversionary attack on Greece.

Personal papers, identifying the body as thirty-six year old Major William Martin, serial number 148228, would also be found on the corpse. And, in case the Germans went to the trouble of finding out whether such a person existed, Intelligence planners built up a detailed biography of Major Martin. Letters from his fictitious fiancée, Pam, were forged. House keys, a bus ticket, a jeweller's receipt for an engagement ring, the stubs of two tickets to a play currently running in the West End, and a rude letter from his bank about a minor overdraft, would also be placed in his pockets, along with a dog-eared photo of 'Pam'.

The final, and most difficult problem, was that of the body itself. It had been decided that the most convincing scenerio would be that Major Martin's transport plane had been shot down in the sea, and, having escaped and donned a lifejacket, he had been drowned by the choppy sea – a frequent occurrence during the war. This meant that they had to find a drowning victim they could pass off as Major Martin – and also, who would have to fulfill the conditions of being Anglo-Saxon in appearance and of the right age.

The Intelligence planners made a search of morgue records, and they were even given permission to raid churchyards. Fortunately, it did not come to that. A civilian of about the right age had recently died in London of pneumonia – which, in its final stages, causes the lungs to fill with water. The man's family were contacted, and the plan explained. Assured that their son would be given a Christian burial in Spain, they agreed. The man (whose name has never been released) had failed the fitness tests for three of the armed forces, but now, as a corpse, was in a position to serve his country.

The 'major' was packed in ice and loaded on to the submarine *Seraph*. On 30 April, the body was dressed, strapped into a Mae West and, briefcase chained to the wrist, lowered into the sea off the south west Spanish coast, near the fishing village of Huelva. Although the tide was favourable, there was no guarantee that Major Martin would reach land before a shark got him. The authorities in London waited anxiously.

A few days later, the Spanish government informed the British Naval Attache in Lisbon that a Royal Marine major called Martin had been washed-up on the Spanish coast. An autopsy had identified the cause of death as 'asphyxiation through immersion in the sea', and the body – minus the briefcase – was delivered to the British vice consul. In

London, after some quiet celebrations, Montagu's team placed an obituary in the *Times,* and asked the vice consul to try and locate the papers, which were of 'great importance and secrecy'. Discreet enquiries were made, and, after two weeks, the case and its contents were delivered to the consulate.

Back in London, the documents were minutely examined by technical experts. They appeared sealed and untampered-with, but under the microscope, minute traps, set when the documents were originally sealed, proved to have been sprung. Somebody had opened, read and resealed the papers. The question was: had the disinformation been passed on to the Nazis?

Spain remained neutral throughout the war, but under Franco's a right-wing military dictatorship, was predictably pro-Axis. The Spanish coast had been chosen for Operation Mincemeat, precisely because the Franco government could be relied on to contravene their neutrality. Now, as preparations for the invasion of Sicily went ahead, British Intelligence found themselves paradoxically hoping they had been betrayed.

On 10 July, 1943, British, United States and Canadian forces invaded Sicily under the command of General Eisenhower — 160,000 men in over 2,000 vessels. The Axis troops were obviously unprepared, and were overwhelmed in a brief, but intense battle.

It was only after the final German defeat in 1945, that the Mincemeat team learned just how successful the operation had been.

Within days of the discovery of Major Martin's body on the beach, photocopies and translations of his documents had been relayed to Berlin. The Germans apparently did not even suspect that it was a trick — the documents looked authentic, and an autopsy revealed that the Martin had died by drowning. After all, it was unlikely that the British had drowned one of their own men to lay a trap. Evaluation

Nazi spies were not all the heartless monsters depicted in the wartime propaganda movies. In fact Hans Schmidt, the most successful Nazi agent to operate in England, is said to have been a rather good-natured soul.

When he and a colleague called Bjornson parachuted near to Salisbury in 1940, the other suffered a severely broken ankle. Standard practice was to leave him and continue the mission alone, but Schmidt refused to abandon his friend. He radioed the situation to Germany and, while waiting for a reply, walked into town and obtained food and basic medical supplies. On his return he was told to leave Bjornson to his fate, but again refused. (It should be noted that he was likely to be shot if captured.) Eventually his bosses gave in and arranged for another agent, already settled in Wales, to collect and nurse the injured Bjornson.

Schmidt got work on a farm in Southern England, fell in love with the farmer's daughter and married her. When not working in the fields, he found time to investigate Allied military movements – including preparations for the Dieppe Raid and D-Day – details of which he duly radioed to Germany. At the end of one message, he astonished his controllers by happily adding that he was now the father of a seven-pound baby boy.

Whereas almost all German spies in Britain were captured during the war, Schmidt continued to operate until V.E. Day – May 7, 1945. After interrogation by MI5, he and his family settled down in London.

reports were swiftly compiled and sent to Admiral Doenitz, Field Marshal Keitel, General Rommel and Adolf Hitler himself. Hitler gave orders that Sardinia should be heavily reinforced. A Panzer division was moved from France, and, ironically, a torpedo boat unit was also sent from Sicily. In their determination to halt the invasion, the Nazis weakened the defences of the island where the Allies actually landed.

Less than a year later, on 4 June, 1944, the Allies entered Rome. To judge purely by results, the unnamed civilian who became Major Martin was the most successful spy of the Second World War.

Lucy from Lucerne

In the early summer of 1941, Britain stood alone against the Nazis. France had fallen, America was declining to become involved in a second European war and Russia, to everyone's astonishment, had signed a pact with their arch enemy Hitler. In retrospect we can see that Stalin was simply playing for time, while Hitler wanted a cover for Operation Barbarossa, his planned blitzkrieg against the Soviet Union. Stalin, on the other hand, signed because he desperately needed time. Belatedly realising that Hitler was not trustworthy, he had ordered a major shake-up in the Soviet military. Although the Red Army was huge, it was outmoded and badly organised — this was largely because Stalin had slaughtered almost the entire officer corps in the purges of the mid 1930s. Replacement officers were inexperienced and nervous.

In May and early June 1941, several sources, including Richard Sorge, informed Moscow Central, the Soviet Intelligence HQ, that the Germans would strike on 15 June. On Stalin's order, these were ignored. One report, however, provided by Englishman Alexander

Foote, provided such precise details of German military dispositions that it caught the attention of senior Russian Intelligence officers. Foote, a member of a Soviet spy ring in Switzerland, explained that he was in contact with an agent – codenamed Lucy – in Lucerne, and that Lucy, in turn, had a contact who was high in the Nazi hierachy.

The Russians felt this was too good to be true but, nevertheless, demanded to know Lucy's identity. Foote apologetically refused, insisting his agent must have total anonymity.

When 15 June passed uneventfully, Stalin informed his advisers that the whole thing had been a plot by Winston Churchill to drag Russia into the war. The Germans, he assured them, would not be able to attack for months or even years, and by then the Red Army would be ready and waiting for them. He was wrong. The Germans had intended to strike on 15 June, but were delayed by an uprising in Yugoslavia. Before a week had passed, Alexander Foote delivered another report from Lucy. The new invasion date was set for 3 am, 22 June, 1941. Stalin tossed the warning aside as he had the previous ones. But the Germans *did* strike that day, and the Soviets were totally unprepared.

In the chaos that followed, Stalin ordered the commander of the western front and his entire staff arrested and shot. More productively, Moscow Central re-examined Lucy's report. Its description and location of the German divisions tallied precisely with the reports sent from the collapsing front. They contacted Foote, and ordered him to go to recruit Lucy at all costs. Stalin, now aware of his stupidity and anxious to make up for it, insisted that Lucy's further cooperation was a top priority. Moscow offered 7,000 Swiss francs a month as a retaining fee to the anonymous agent – the highest payment to any Soviet spy throughout the war.

Lucy then produced a stream of military information so highly detailed that it might have been sent by Hitler himself. Not only were there minute descriptions of the type and disposition of the advancing German army, but also the condition and future plans of the Luftwaffe and the German Navy (including the highly secret moves of the U-boat wolf-packs). Lucy's contacts, whoever they were, could only have been located in either the O.K.W. (Oberkommando Wehrmacht), the headquarters of the German High Command, or Hitler's own bunker staff. Only in these places could such varied information come together.

By now it was clear that the contact could not be a subversive file clerk or a general's secretary. The top secret information, such as the V-1 rocket bomb project, meant that the spy had to be, at the very least, a major general.

Stalin is said to have avidly read each new Lucy report, and regulated his troop movements accordingly. But although the bulletins proved accurate again and again, they were not enough to turn the tide of Russian defeat. The German panzer divisions roared eastward, and the battered Russians were driven back. Knowing the precise make up and disposition of the enemy forces was little more than salt on the Red Army's wounds, since they had neither the equipment or organisation to counter them. Through the summer and autumn of 1941, as the Germans captured an area many times larger that their own country, they were astounded at the Soviet's casualness about their own troops. By the end of September, nearly three million had been sacrificed to cover what amounted to a mass retreat. How long, Hitler wondered aloud, could the Russians survive such punishment before surrendering?

But Stalin had his own plan. Thanks to Lucy. German supply lines were being stretched to their limit by the swift advance and, in their over-confidence, the O.K.W. had neglected to outfit their troops with winter clothing and equipment. The Fuhrer himself had insisted that the campaign would be over before the first snows, and even his military experts, who knew better, dared not question his word. Indeed, when a panzer commander radioed to ask about winter supplies, he was told not waste time with frivolous requests. This lack of planning was duly passed on by Lucy, and Stalin bided his time.

On 10 October, 1942, the first snow fell. By mid November the temperature had dropped to minus forty degrees centigrade and the oil in the German transports and weapons froze solid. The German soldiers, wearing only summer uniforms, began to fall to frostbite like flies. Finally, on 6 December, with Nazi troops within fifteen miles of Moscow, the Russians struck back.

The Siberian divisions — elite troops, specifically equipped and trained for Russian winter conditions — had been held in reserve. (Richard Sorge's report that the Japanese were intent only on war in the Pacific had freed these troops from guarding the eastern frontier.) Now they drove the demoralised Germans back from Moscow, just as they had driven the French under Napoleon a hundred and thirty years previously. It was the beginning of the long and bloody Soviet advance that would eventually end in Berlin.

For the next two years, Lucerne Lucy provided the Soviets with superb, up-to-the-minute military data. Armed with this information, the Russians were able to strike at the Nazis' weakest flanks or lay traps for enemy offensives at will. The Russian Front became such a death trap that Germans nicknamed it 'the mass grave'. Time and again, the German commanders ordered a blitzkrieg pincer attack (the Wehrmacht's speciality) only to find the Russian armies had melted-away as if by magic. In their attempts to counter the sheer mass of the Russian army, the Germans were forced to spread themselves thin on the eastern front. By the end of 1943, most Allied military experts agreed that the Nazis could not win the war in the east.

In early 1944, the Lucy reports stopped. The reason, it emerged later, was the arrest by the Swiss authorities of both Alexander Foote and agent Lucy on spying charges. Switzerland was, of course, a neutral country, but we now know that Swiss Secret Service knew about and even assisted Lucy's mission while the war went the Nazis' way. There was little doubt that Hitler would try to invade the mountain state sooner or later, and as long as the Russians held out, it was likely to be later. However, when it became plain that Hitler was losing the war, the Swiss reverted to a stricter definition of neutrality.

The arrests were strictly for Foote and Lucy's protection. The Germans were well-aware that a traitor was giving away their top military secrets – inefficient Russian commanders had twice allowed transcripts of Lucy reports to be left behind during hasty strategic withdrawals. Using radio tracking and an agonisingly slow search of the wavebands, the Sicherheitsdienst – the Nazi party's own secret service – managed to detect Foote's radio broadcasts to Moscow. Although they could decode only a tiny amount of the nightly reports, it became plain that they contained detailed military information. Triangulation of the transmission source revealed it to be located in Switzerland, so Nazi agents were flooded into that country to find and stop the leak. Realising what was happening, the Swiss authorities found Lucy and his radio operator first, and placed them in protective custody. This was not entirely a selfless act: the Swiss remembered that the invasion of Holland had been ordered by Hitler on the pretext that the Dutch had harboured just two British spies.

Agent Lucy was revealed to be a middle-aged publisher called Rudolf Roessler. A native Bavarian, Roessler had fought with distinction in the German army during World War I. Following the defeat, he left the military and became a journalist, but remained in contact with the young officers with whom he had served. Although a right winger,

The brutality of the Gestapo in occupied France reached savage proportions, but in Toulouse in 1943, the tables were turned on them. Marcel Taillandier, head of a Resistance group that was constantly losing people to betrayal and arrest, decided to strike back directly. Not only French quislings, but Gestapo men themselves were targeted. Prominent officers were shot down in the street in broad daylight. Others went to meet with contacts only to be kidnapped, tortured and killed. Within three months, the Toulouse Gestapo were effectively under siege – hardly daring to meet with even their most trusted informers.

As Nazi arrogance was curbed, the Resistance fighters took greater and greater risks. At one point, Taillandier even managed to infiltrate the Gestapo himself, feeding them false information and leading them on a wild-goose chase after a non-existent Resistance group.

The pinnacle of Taillandier's campaign came on New Year's Day, 1944, when a secret Gestapo convoy of trucks was ambushed. The escort and guards were killed and scores of files detailing suspected Resistance fighters were captured. By alerting people that they were under suspicion, Taillandier's group saved hundreds of lives.

In July, 1944, Taillandier was himself caught. He tried to escape, but was seriously wounded and rushed to a hospital. Within hours he was removed by Gestapo officers and was never seen alive again. That night the Gestapo held a

champagne banquet to celebrate. A few weeks
later, when they were forced to flee by the
advancing Allies, Marcel Taillandier's viciously
mutilated corpse was found buried in the garden
of the Gestapo building.

Roessler hated Nazism with a passion that eventually made
it unsafe for him to remain in Germany. He and his wife
arrived in Lucerne shortly after Hitler's rise to power and
set up a publishing business specialising in anti-Nazi books.
He still maintained contact with his army friends in
Germany, and it was two of these, by then generals in
the Wehrmacht, who approached him in May 1937, with
the idea of striking at Nazism from the inside.

These generals represented eight other officers – three
generals, a colonel, a major and three captains – all of whom
worked in the O.K.W. HQ in Berlin. Seeing the inevitable
slide into war, they had decided to betray their homeland's
secrets with the sole aim of destroying the Nazis. From
1939 onwards, these men used the O.K.W.'s own radio
centre to transmit nightly, encoded reports to Roessler in
Switzerland. The radio traffic out of the Wehrmacht HQ
was so heavy that the risk of their being discovered was
next to nil.

Roessler first approached the Swiss authorities with his
mine of information but, although grateful, they could do
little with it, and were afraid of passing it on to the Allies in
case they were discovered in major breach of their neutrality. But they told him he was free to do as he wished –
provided he was careful. Being essentially anti-Communist,
his next preference was for the French and British. These
accepted his reports but discounted them as too good to be
true. Three months before the Germans made their surprise
attack through the forested Sedan Gap into France, Roessler

had passed on their full battle order to the Allies. These were never read and France collapsed within weeks. It is an unpalatable fact that if the western allies had listened to Roessler, the war could have been won in 1940. Disgusted by this stupidity, he finally turned to the Soviets and, through a communist friend, contacted Alexander Foote.

After arresting them, the Swiss held Roessler and Foote for several months until the danger had passed. During this time a group of German officers attempted to kill Hitler in a bomb plot. Hitler survived the blast, the plot failed and the resultant witchhunt conducted by the Gestapo reached to the very top of the German High Command. Hundreds of officers were executed on the slightest hint of a connection with the conspiracy, often with their entire families. Roessler returned to his transmitter haunted by fear for his friends. After a nerve-racking two weeks of silence, his radio messages were answered. All ten of the traitors were alive. They had assiduously avoided contact with the clumsy bomb-plotters and remained in their positions in the O.K.W.

But the Lucy Ring was no longer needed. When Foote re-contacted Moscow on Roessler's behalf, Russian Intelligence replied that further reports were unnecessary — victory over Germany was fully assured. This rejection seems to have broken something inside Roessler; one day he had been driven by the conviction that he was saving civilization, and the next told he was surplus to requirements.

The Russians certainly had no intention of thanking him or even acknowledging the enormous part he and his friends had played in defeating Hitler. Stalin was now claiming to be the sole architect of the Russian victory, had no intention of sharing the glory. Two members of Foote's spy ring, for example, were secretly thrown into a Siberian gulag for twelve years when they returned to Russia, for fear they might reveal what they knew about agent Lucy.

The ten traitors dropped out of sight after the war, probably relieved to be still alive, and all Roessler's efforts to re-contact them proved useless. Rudolf Roessler died in 1957, an embittered man. He took the names of his compatriots with him to the grave.

Chapter Four

THE ATOM SPIES

A t dawn on 16 July, 1945, the first atom bomb was detonated in the Alamogordo desert, New Mexico. As the dust cloud mushroomed into the sky before them, the scientists of the Manhattan Project watched with as much fear as exultation – there was, they knew, a remote chance that the atomic chain reaction could continue and eventually set the planet's entire atmosphere on fire. It was probably then that someone coined the phrase 'Doomsday scenario'.

The US Army generals running the project had been informed of the risk, but when they were also told that it might take the physicists more than a week to study the problem and resolve the ambiguity, they insisted the test take place as planned. They were under political pressure to have the bomb available as soon as possible.

Britain and America had been jointly working on the Manhattan Project – codenamed the Tube Alloys Project by the British – since 1941. Canada was also involved, but the Soviet Union was not told what was happening. The original target for the bomb was Berlin (it was not known for some time whether the Germans were ahead or behind the Allies in building an atomic device). But by the time the project reached completion, the Nazis had surrendered and it was the Japanese who were targeted.

It has been alleged that the reason the generals were in such a hurry to test the bomb was that they feared Japan would surrender before it could be used – the implication being that the bomb was not wanted to end the war, but to terrify the Russians, and that the destruction of one or two

Atomic Bomb Test in New Mexico, 1945

cities was the only way to bring the weapon's full implications home to the 'Red Menace'. In fact, there is very little evidence to back this bleakly cynical view. The generals were mainly under pressure because President Truman hoped the bomb would save the lives of thousands of American GI's, expected to be lost in the storming of the Japanese islands.

Even so, it can hardly be doubted that President Truman was aware of the political leverage the bomb would offer in the negotiations with Stalin.

Truman, Stalin and Churchill ('the big three') had met in Potsdam, Berlin on 15 July, 1945, to discuss the future position of European political boundaries. Although he had been informed that the bomb worked, President Truman was conciliatory to the Soviets' aggressive demands up to 21 July, when he became noticeably more assertive and firm. The reason was that he had read a full report of the bomb's effect and was reassured that he had an unbeatable card up his sleeve. At the close of negotiations on 24 July, Truman took Stalin to one side and informed him of the American development of an atom bomb. To the president's surprise Stalin simply replied, unemotionally, that he hoped that United States would make good use of the weapon. Truman had hoped for some sign of shock or alarm. Speaking with Churchill later, he could only suggest that Stalin was so ignorant that he did not realise the sheer destructive power of an atomic bomb.

We now know that the reverse was the case. Soviet spies had been reporting on the Manhattan Project from the beginning, and had infiltrated it to its very core. Stalin did not react to the news of the bomb because he did not want to give the Americans any clue that he already knew all about their secret weapon. But a secret of these proportions was almost impossible to keep. Within two months the western Allies were getting their first inkling of the biggest espionage coup in history.

Churchill, Truman and Stalin at the Potsdam Conference, 1945

Igor Gouzenko

By the evening of 6 September, 1945, a few months after the unconditional surrender of Nazi Germany, Russian diplomat Igor Gouzenko felt that he was under sentence of death. He had attempted to betray his country and defect to the west; but now it seemed the west did not want him, or worse, couldn't be bothered to find out what he wanted. The two men who were watching his apartment from the bench across the road were almost certainly Soviet secret police. If he were lucky, he thought, they might just shoot him and get it over with.

Gouzenko had never been considered a security risk by his superiors at the Soviet embassy in Ottawa. Born in 1919, he had joined the Young Communist League at seventeen and throughout his schooling and subsequent attendance at the Moscow Engineering Academy, he had show enthusiasm for the Party and all it stood for. His political fervour and skill as an electrical engineer came to the attention of talent scouts for the NKVD (later known as the KGB) and he had been transferred from the academy to the security service General Staff School. Graduating in late 1941, he was posted to the Main Intelligence Division of the Red Army, and served a year on the western front during the invasion of Russia.

When he returned from the war, he was picked out for service abroad. This, in so young an agent, was high praise – the paranoid Stalin felt that regular contact with the outside world threatened the loyalty of Soviet citizens.

Being chosen was only the first step. Next he had to undergo thorough surveillance. His behaviour and habits were closely scrutinised, and lengthy reports were compiled under the headings: sexual weaknesses, alcohol intake, financial stability, tendency towards talking too much, and observance of security regulations. Since Gouzenko was aware he was on trial – and the watchers knew he knew

– any slip during that half year would have meant he would be barred from working for any branch of the NKVD. Finally, he was passed as secure.

Lieutenant Gouzenko, with his wife and small son, was sent to the Soviet embassy in Canada, where he was given the position of cipher clerk on the staff of the military attache, Colonel Zabotin. As a cipher clerk, Gouzenko saw every message that went in and out of the NKVD operation in Ottawa, and soon realised his chief must be running one of the biggest spy rings in the western hemisphere. Over the next two years, Gouzenko worked conscientiously, and gave Zabotin no cause for concern. Yet the young Russian was becoming more and more enamoured of life in the west. Since he was officially a civilian employee, he and his family were allowed to live outside the embassy complex in a pleasant apartment. There was virtually no food rationing, and because the Soviet Union was on the side of the west, all the Canadians he met treated him with expansive friendliness. Ottawa was certainly preferable to miserable shortage-bound Moscow, with its constant fear of political purges.

As time went on he 'forgot to destroy' certain interesting documents that crossed his desk, hiding them away for possible future use. Yet he still wavered when it came to actually betraying his fellow countrymen. Finally, it was an unexpected recall to Russia that forced him to make a decision. It might be a routine re-posting; on the other hand, it might be his death-warrant. Possibly someone had noticed that he was failing to destroy documents. Even after the end of the war, people were still being liquidated in Stalin's Russia.

Taking his collection of over a hundred documents and messages, Gouzenko left work at the usual time on 5 September, 1945. He went straight to one of Canada's leading newspapers, the *Ottawa Journal*. There he told the news editor that he wanted political asylum from the Soviet

Union and had with him documents of the highest importance to the Canadian government. The newsman glanced at the documents and pointed-out that they were in Russian. Yes, replied Gouzenko, that was rather the point. 'I can't read Russian', countered the ace reporter, 'why don't you go to the Royal Canadian Mounted Police?'

Bewildered and frightened, Gouzenko found himself bundled out the newspaper's front door like some lunatic inventor. He then hurried across town to the Ministry of Justice but, it then being close to midnight, was told by the doorman to come back in the morning. Returning to his apartment he had to tell his heavily pregnant wife that their plan to escape had to be postponed until the next day. Neither of them slept well that night.

Gouzenko was moderately certain that his Russian colleagues were unaware of what he had in mind. He had been trained in noticing surveillance men, and was fairly sure he had not been followed the night before. But if he failed to turn up at work the following day, his absence would be noted and investigated. That meant he had to try either defecting a second time, or go to work as usual. He decided to take the risk and try again, aware that if he failed a second time, he and his wife would probably not survive the day.

The next morning, accompanied by his family, he went back to Ministry of Justice. At the enquiries desk he asked to see the minister but, predictably, was told he would have to apply for an appointment and come back another day. After much fuss and argument, Gouzenko was finally shown upstairs to the minister's secretary. He explained, with growing impatience, that he was a Soviet intelligence officer who was willing to tell everything he knew in return for political asylum. The secretary listened with much the same ironic amusement as the editor of the *Ottawa Journal*, then picked up the phone and talked to the minister. The conversation was in French, a language Gouzenko did not understand, but he guessed before the secretary hung up that he was going to get another polite brush off.

Why was Gouzenko having such trouble defecting? With the knowledge of forty years of the Cold War behind us, it seems ridiculous that he was not instantly granted asylum. But this is to overlook the fact that, in 1945, the Russians and the Western allies had just jointly won the war, and on the part of the West, there was a state of glowing euphoria and trust. There was also the fact that, although defections from the enemy had occasionally happened, defection from an ally was simply unheard of. Gouzenko and his family were the first cold war defectors. Unfortunately, it looked as if no one wanted them.

After trying the *Ottawa Journal* again, to no avail, and unsuccessfuly applying for Canadian citizenship, the Gouzenkos returned gloomily to their apartment. The sun was setting, and Igor left his tearful family to meditate on his options on the balcony. His conclusion was that his only way of saving his family was to hand himself over to the NKVD.

Now it so happened that on the adjoining balcony, his neighbours, Royal Canadian Air Force Sergeant Harold Main and his wife, were also taking the evening air. Gouzenko told them everything and begged them, if he handed himself over to the NKVD, to get his wife and son away to safety. Sgt.Main was horrified. He insisted the whole family come into his apartment while he rang the police. Two uniformed officers duly arrived and promised to watch the apartment block through the night. Unfortunately, they said, it was not in their power to do any more.

Peering through a crack in the Main's curtains, Gouzenko observed two strangers in greatcoats take up position on the bench opposite his flat, and knew the NKVD were on to him. At midnight somebody battered in the door of the Gouzenkos' empty apartment. The two Canadian policemen arrived moments later and questioned the intruders.

They freely gave their identities as members of the Soviet delegation, and claimed diplomatic immunity. Comrade Gouzenko, they said, had absconded with a great deal of money belonging to the Soviet people and they were only seeking to apprehend him. When the policemen pressed further questions the NKVD agents haughtily started to leave. Impressed by their air of confidence, the officers did not try to stop them. Looking through the next-door letter slot, Gouzenko recognised embassy security chief Pavlov among the Russians, and all but gave up hope. If Pavlov was willing to risk arrest for breaking and entering, it meant the NKVD was determined catch him.

In fact, Pavlov had just saved Gouzenko's life. From the time Gouzenko left the Minister of Justice's outer-office, the Canadians had been following the would-be defector. Indeed, the two men on the bench opposite the apartment building were not NKVD men, but non-uniform members of the Royal Canadian Mounted Police. The authorities had not been sure what to do with Gouzenko, and were very nervous of falling into some sort of diplomatic trap. Following the conversation with his secretary, the Minister of Justice ordered the Canadian MI5 to wait 24-hours before even considering making official contact with Gouzenko. Now that Pavlov had revealed himself so desperate to recapture the cipher clerk, they felt certain that Gouzenko was genuine. By the next morning the family were in protective custody and had been granted political asylum.

The relieved Gouzenko was subjected to over a week of non-stop interrogation. (During that time his wife gave birth in a military hospital with a Mountie sergeant masquerading as the proud father.) A fortnight after the defector had first been given asylum, Prime Minister Mackenzie-King was briefed concerning his revelations. He learned that Colonel Zabotin, the Soviet military attache, was running a huge spy ring, codenamed 'the

Net'. The Russians had infiltrated Canadian government and military organisations and were obtaining secret information with frightening ease. What was worse, the Net crossed borders. Based in the Soviet embassy in Ottawa, the spy ring had many contacts in both Britain and America. These nations would need to be informed at once.

When he set-up the Net, Zabotin had only employed hard core Canadian communists, regardless of their ability to actually obtain secrets. These were his corps of scouts and recruiters. They would look for people with left wing sympathies in important positions and report on them to Zabotin. He and his agents would then carry out an in-depth check on the target, looking for a weakness. Were they in financial difficulties? Did they have a lover they would rather not have exposed? Did they harbour some grudge against the authorities? An angle was found, and the best way to approach them decided. If the person seemed the nervous type, a fellow Canadian was sent. If they seemed the sort who relished adventure or were enthusiastically pro-Soviet, Colonel Zabotin would contact them himself. If an agent could not be recruited in a key department, members of the spy ring in other areas of government would pull strings to get one of their own a job there. In this way, the Net had thoroughly infiltrated the Canadian state apparatus.

Yet more insidious was Zabotin's creation of what MI5 call 'illegals'. Even rabid pro-Communists would stop short of doing major damage to their own country. In certain circumstances, however, Zabotin needed Canadian citizens whose only loyalty was to the USSR. Russian NKVD agents, trained to pass as Canadian nationals, were smuggled into the country and given false documentation by Net agents in the Home Office. Thanks to the confusion of war, when these illegals claimed to have moved from another part of the country, nobody checked their state-

Canadian Prime Minister, Mackenzie-King

ments. They then infiltrated the areas in which natural Canadians were less willing to spy, such as the military.

The Net's orders from Moscow Central were to obtain information on more than two dozen different areas of interest, ranging from troop movements to chemical plant systems. At the top of this list was infiltration of the Chalk River uranium processing plant in Ontario. On hearing this, Prime Minister Mackenzie-King asked shakily if the Manhattan Project had been compromised. In reply he was handed a copy of a message from Zabotin to the 'Director' in Moscow. It passed on precise details, obtained from an agent codenamed 'Alek', of the uranium and plutonium composition of the atomic bombs dropped on Hiroshima and Nagasaki. The way it was phrased made it perfectly clear that the Russians had a good working understanding of the bomb's mechanisms. Furthermore, it stated that Alek had obtained a 162 microgram sample of uranium 235 from the Chalk River plant, and that this was on its way to the scientists in Moscow by special courier. The subtext of the message was that the Soviets not only knew all about the workings of the atom bomb, but were developing one of their own.

Mackenzie-King was understandably shattered by Gouzenko's evidence. It was clearly an urgent duty to inform the governments of Britain and America what was happening, but he decided he could not rely on the usual methods of communication. It was still not known who could be trusted in the government departments. (Everyone mentioned in Net messages was referred to by codename, even doormen and chauffeurs.) He flew to Washington then London to personally pass on the bad news. Both President Truman and the new British Prime Minister, Clement Attlee were deeply upset by the revelations. The Soviet betrayal of friendship, discovered hardly a month after the Japanese surrender, totally destroyed the hope that the Allies might maintain the wartime bonds. They were feeling the first chill of the coming Cold War.

Allan Nunn May

The Canadian authorities were in no hurry to arrest those few they could identify as Net spies. In counter-espionage, a free agent is more likely to lead you to his associates than a jailed one. However one spy, agent 'Alek', had to be identified and stopped as soon as possible. The leak of atomic secrets was to be plugged, even if doing so alerted every other Net agent.

The fact that he or she could lay their hands on a small sample of uranium 235, the nuclear material used in the bomb, offered little clue to Alek's identity. A reasonably adventurous lab cleaner might have been able to do it. On the other hand, the precise details of the bombs dropped over Japan, given in the Zabotin message, suggested Alek was a scientist or top military bureaucrat. Fortunately for the Canadians, there was another Alek message from Zabotin to the Director in Gouzenko's collection of papers. The colonel warned Moscow that Alek would be forced to return to London in September. This pointed to Alek being a British member of the Manhattan Project. Since Zabotin also mentioned Alek would be working at King's College in the Strand, and most of the British contingent in the USA were scientists, Alek was almost certainly not a bureaucrat. A quick check of scientists from the bomb project who had returned to Britain in September, cross-indexed with the faculty register at King's College pointed conclusively to one man: Dr Allan Nunn May.

Nunn May was a small, balding man with steel-rimmed glasses and a Hitler moustache. He had occupied an important post in the Manhattan Project and had worked on a number of occasions at the Chalk River uranium processing plant. This, of course, did not prove his guilt. Although MI5 were certain that the Zabotin message was genuine – as opposed to a plant aimed at incriminating an innocent man – they would still have to catch Nunn May red-handed or force a confession out of him if they were to convince a jury.

Arresting Nunn May in the act of espionage was the most favoured course. Since Gouzenko's defection, the Net had effectively gone to ground, but did not seem to have shut down permanently. Zabotin knew Gouzenko must have taken files with him, but since most of the information that had crossed the defector's desk had supposedly been 'burned for security reasons', he had no idea what information the Canadians now possessed. If an important agent like Nunn May was arrested and grilled for no apparent reason, Colonel Zabotin would guess how far he had been compromised and initiate escape and deep-cover procedures for his remaining agents. On the other hand, if Nunn May could be caught in a blatant act of espionage, Zabotin would not be too alarmed – indeed, it would be in his interest to remain calm. The fact that the Net was still running suggested that the Colonel had down-played the importance of Gouzenko's defection in his reports to Moscow Central. But If he suddenly closed down the spy ring, he would almost certainly face a court-martial for incompetence.

Nunn May was placed under round-the-clock observation, and his background re-examined. It made embarrassing reading for the British security services. Born the son of a moderately well-off Birmingham brass founder, Nunn May had a brilliant career at Cambridge, eventually becoming a Doctor of Philosophy (specialising in Einsteinian physics) in 1936. Throughout his time at the university, Nunn May had made no secret of his pronounced left wing sympathies. Shortly after securing his doctorate, he spent several weeks visiting Leningrad. There was no particular evidence that he was recruited by the Russians at this time, but the trip should have been thoroughly investigated when he was vetted for the bomb-project, and it was not.

When he returned to Britain, Nunn May had joined the editorial board of the *Scientific Worker*, the magazine for the National Association of Scientific Workers. The Association was not openly pro-Soviet, but had leftish tendencies, and some members were openly pro-Communist. Shortly before the outbreak of the war, Nunn May was appointed to a scientific teaching position at London University which meant that he was automatically excused military service. In early Summer, 1942, he was approached by Sir Wallace Ackers of ICI and asked to help with the Tube Alloys Project (the British nuclear program). Nunn May was, of course, security checked by MI5 for such top secret work, but despite his openly pro-Communist sympathies, he was not even called for an interview.

The fact that Russia had just come into the war on the side of the Allies meant that not even MI5 wanted to think of the USSR as a potential enemy. It was an often-quoted epigram of the time that anyone below thirty who is not a left winger has no heart, and that anyone above forty who is not a right winger has no head. It was no secret that many leading figures in the corridors of power had flirted with communism in their university days. If this was to become a reason to deny security access, MI5 reasoned, there wouldn't be enough people to run the country, let alone the war. Unfortunately, in the face of the Nunn May revelations, this argument was beginning to sound decidedly hollow.

In January, 1943, Alan Nunn May had been one of the first group of British scientists to be sent to North America to co-operate on the Manhattan Project. The Gouzenko papers reveal that he was contacted by a Soviet agent very shortly after his arrival, which suggests that he had already been recruited on the British side of the Atlantic. Set to work in the Chicago laboratory, one of the major nerve-centres of the project, Nunn May threw himself into the work. He took an interest in everything going on in the lab, whether it involved his part of the project or not. By the time of the Alamogordo test, he was generally regarded as the best-informed British atomic scientist outside the project base at Los Alamos. Nunn May's regular visits to the Chalk River uranium processing plant were regarded as another aspect of his polymathic interests – colleagues and security personnel indulged his curiosity.

The Gouzenko papers revealed that, following Nunn May's return to Britain, he was due to meet with a Soviet contact-man outside the British Museum on 17 October, 1945. At eight o'clock in the evening, Nunn May was to stroll down Great Russell Street with a copy of the *Times* under his left arm. The Soviet agent would approach from the other direction with a *Picture Post* in his left hand. The Russian would make first contact with the words; 'What is the shortest way to the Strand?'

Nunn May was to answer: 'Well, come along, I am going that way.'

To show it was safe to discuss business Nunn May should then say; 'Best regards from Mikel.'

It was a classic, well planned piece of spycraft, but if Nunn May went though with it, MI5 would be able to identify and tail his contact-man. Sooner or later, they knew, Nunn May would be want to hand over more nuclear secrets. The moment anything that could contain paper-work was passed from him to his contact, Special Branch would pounce.

17 October came and went without Nunn May going anywhere near the British Museum. Neither were there any Russians seen wandering about Great Russell Street clutch-ing copies of *Picture Post*. Although Zabotin's orders were for the meeting to be attempted on the same day and hour

of each month until contact was made, Nunn May pointedly stuck to his normal routine. He had clearly been warned, but whether it was by some unknown traitor in British Intelligence, or whether Colonel Zabotin had managed to put out a general alert, was unknown.

By 15 February, 1946, the Canadian authorities had identified enough of the codenamed traitors to strike. They had to forgo the pleasure of deporting Colonel Zabotin, since he had already bolted back to Russia at the turn of the year (where he was given a four year jail sentence for failing to spot the traitor in his organisation). The blitzkrieg of arrests was not as great a surprise to the remaining Net agents as the authorities had hoped – the US news media had broadcast the discovery of a major Soviet spy ring in Canada, twelve days earlier. Perhaps because of this forewarning, only eighteen arrests were made.

On the same day in England, Dr Nunn May was asked to attend a meeting at the British Atomic Energy Authority at Shell-Mex House. He went without suspecting trouble, having been often called to such meetings, but this time was surprised to be introduced to Commander Leonard Burt, Chief of Special Branch.

Burt opened the discussion by pointedly telling Nunn May that a serious leak of atomic information had taken place in Canada. The doctor replied, unruffled; 'It's news to me. It's the first I've heard of it.'

The commander pressed on. British Intelligence, he said, had reason to suspect that Nunn May had dealt with a certain Colonel Zabotin of the NKVD. Nunn May denied this categorically. The rest of the interview followed the same pattern. Whatever line of questioning Burt tried, Nunn May coolly denied it. Finally, showing a fine instinct for interrogation, Burt turned the situation on its head. Would Nunn May, he asked, be willing to provide help and information for the British security forces to use against the Soviet Union? For the first time, the doctor was caught off guard.

'Not if it is to be used in counter-espionage', he replied, after a confused pause.

Burt terminated the interview shortly before midnight. A search of Nunn May's flat and his person revealed nothing. Nevertheless, although the commander had failed to obtain a confession, he had the next best thing: a certainty that Nunn May was guilty. The doctor had inadvertently shown a deep conflict of interests when asked to act against Russia — and what was more, he clearly knew that Burt had noted it.

Unhurried now, since they were certain the scientist would not dare try to pass on more secrets, MI5 watched their suspect and let him stew in his own juice. After a few days they called him in for a second questioning. Nunn May was clearly suffering for the strain; even before he sat down he tremulously complained that he was being followed. Burt casually turned to his subordinate and told him be more circumspect in the future. Nunn May reacted angrily, but his bluster could not conceal his fright. It was becoming clear to him that the authorities were not going to give up. It was only a matter of time before they broke his resistance, and both he and they knew it.

Seeing that Nunn May's resolve was finally cracking, Commander Burt pressed him hard. He demanded to be told why the scientist had failed to meet his Soviet contact outside the British Museum. Nunn May started to deny any such meeting had been arranged, but Burt continued, peppering him with the planned details of the rendezvous, including the recognition phrases. Seeing how much the police knew, Nunn May's resolve broke and he asked to make a full confession.

But the statement was obviously well-prepared, suggesting trained preparation. He named no names and tried to reduce his espionage activities to a bare minimum. When asked why he had betrayed his country, he replied stiffly that he had felt it a great wrong to hide vital information from a wartime ally. The decision to feed atomic secrets to the Russians was a very painful one, he conceded, but it had been the only course his conscience could allow.

Dr Allan Nunn May was tried at Old Bailey in March 1946. Since it was competing with the Nuremberg war crime trials for headline space, the case received remarkably little publicity. When the Attorney General read out the charge that Nunn May had broken the Official Secrets Act by passing information 'calculated to be directly or indirectly useful to an enemy', he felt it necessary to explain that this was merely the official form of the charge. Nobody, he stressed, wanted to suggest that the Soviet Union was, or potentially could be, Britain's enemy.

Nunn May was found guilty and given ten years, but was released in 1952 for good behaviour. Not surprisingly, he found it hard to find work worthy of his abilities, but persisted and soon articles under his name were appearing in *Nature*, the organ of the scientific establishment. In 1962, he and his family emigrated to Ghana in West Africa, where he became Professor of Physics at the state university.

Klaus Fuchs

Although deeply embarrassed by the Nunn May revelations, British Intelligence felt they had at least some cause for self-congratulation. From what the scientist was known to have told the Soviets about the atom bomb, it was estimated that it would still take them until at least 1953 to develop their own weapon. The Americans had recruited the finest physicists in the world for the Manhattan Project. The Russians, despite their stolen information, must still be lagging far behind the west in atomic physics.

Considering how much the western atom spies did to fuel the nuclear arms race, it is strange to note that it was a Soviet traitor who almost certainly saved the world from nuclear war.

Oleg Penkovsky was a Colonel in the GRU (Soviet military intelligence) when he approached the British Secret Service in 1961. They could hardly believe their luck – here, at last, was contact as high in the Russian hierarchy as Donald Maclean had been in the British Foreign Office. Penkovsky – codenamed 'Hero' by his delighted controllers – was motivated by the conviction that Russian Premier Khrushchev's aggressive posturing was going push America into World War III. By offering evidence that the USSR was unprepared to fight a nuclear war, Penkovsky hoped to cool western fears.

Over the following year, agent Hero provided the stunning truth behind Soviet propaganda. Khrushchev had claimed well over a thousand intercontinental nuclear missiles – Penkovsky produced proof that the Russians had between ten and fifty in working order at any one time. (Of course, ten would still be enough to devastate the US eastern seaboard or western Europe).

During the Cuba Missile Crisis in 1962 – when the Soviets insisted that they had no missiles stationed in the Caribbean – Hero desperately warned that they had. If US President Kennedy ordered the invasion of Cuba, said Penkovsky, the Soviets would launch. Kennedy agonised for

two days, then decided to follow the advice of
the Russian traitor over that of the Pentagon
generals. The world stepped back from the
brink of nuclear war.

Sad to say, Penkovsky earned no reward for
saving mankind. The British Secret Service
overworked him, he became sloppy and was
arrested by the GRU. After a public show trial
he was sentenced to death and shot on 16 May,
1963.

When, on 23 September, 1949, President Truman announced that the Soviet Union had successfully exploded
an atom bomb, it was clear to everyone in the US and
British security services that another Soviet agent must
have been feeding nuclear information to the enemy, and a
full-scale investigation was just gaining momentum, on
both sides of the Atlantic, when a totally unexpected
source provided the name of the traitor.

In 1939, Finnish intelligence had managed to lay their
hands on a set of NKVD code books. These had eventually
been acquired by the Americans who had put them to
immediate use, decoding messages eavesdropped from the
Soviet embassy in Washington (duplicity against allies
was not confined to the Russians during the war). The
operation, codename Venona, collected a vast pile of
correspondence before the unsuspecting Soviets routinely
changed their codes. Unfortunately for the Americans, it
was a painfully slow and haphazard process to unscramble
the messages without the correct deciphering machine.
Until at least part of the code was cracked in each case, it
was not apparent whether the message was important or
routine, and it was necessary to trawl through large
amounts of relatively trivial information to filter out

what they were looking for. Therefore, the decoding of two messages concerning the second traitor, only shortly after his existence was discovered, was a remarkable stroke of good luck.

If the discovery of Nunn May's treachery had been an embarrassment for British Intelligence, the revelation that Dr Klaus Fuchs was a Soviet spy was more of a moral blow. Although a German, Fuchs had thrown himself into the Tube Alloys Project since its inception in 1941. Subsequently he had been one of the most valuable scientists donated by Britain to the Manhattan Project. After the war he had been offered a high security posting to Harwell, Britain's main nuclear research facility. To his friends, he had been the personification of international co-operation on the bomb project. Yet now Venona made it plain that he had for years been providing the Soviets with every detail of the project that passed through his hands. In fact, in the light of the detailed instructions he had passed on, the real mystery was why the Russians had taken so long to build and detonate their own device.

It took MI5 comparatively little time to trick Fuchs into confession. Security at Harwell reported that the scientist seemed to be suffering some sort of mental crisis, so when Special Branch officer Jim Skardon was despatched there in late 1949, he was ordered to proceed very gently. After the first interview, Skardon – who had been told nothing of the Venona revelations – reported that Fuchs was indeed unhappy, but did not appear to be a traitor. He was told to persist and, by Christmas, 1950, had managed to win Fuchs' trust and friendship. The police officer told Fuchs that all might be forgiven if he came clean about his Soviet contacts. The scientist, who had been agonising over his espionage role since the reported detonation of the Soviet bomb, broke down and made a full confession.

Reading Fuchs' statement Richard White, Head of MI5, is said to have expressed sympathy for the traitor. It seemed, he said, that Fuchs had gone wrong through trying to serve too many causes, rather than because of the spy's usual tendency to betray one to the other.

Fuchs was born in 1911 near Frankfurt. His father was a highly moral man, a Lutheran pastor who had barely escaped conviction by the Nazis on a charge of subversion in 1932. Sealing his own political fate at university in the same year, Klaus Fuchs joined a communist student organisation and engaged in street fighting with Nazi brownshirts – on one occasion being almost beaten to death. While recovering, he was warned he was about to be arrested by the Gestapo and fled first to France and then England. British customs questioned him when he registered as a foreign national, but he managed to avoid mentioning his membership of the German Communist Party. Settling with the friend of a friend in Somerset, he returned to his interrupted study of theoretical physics and made no effort to contact the British Communists. His brilliance soon won the quiet young man a place in Bristol University and by 1938, he had acquired doctorates in both philosophy and science. He was respected by his fellow physicists and, with their support, applied for British citizenship in the summer of 1939. His days of political activism seemed long behind him as he looked forward to a career in the world of theoretical physics.

At the outbreak of war, his adopted country had declared him an enemy alien, and he was shipped to an internment camp in Canada which happened to be full of Nazi supporters. Lonely and isolated, he was delighted to meet a fellow left winger named Hans Kahle. Although Fuchs later denied it, Kahle, a veteran of the Spanish Civil War with connections in the NKVD, was probably the man who

Dr Klaus Fuchs

recruited him to the Soviet cause. After a miserable six months, Fuchs was finally released – due to pressure from friends in the scientific community. Two months after his return to Britain, he was approached by fellow German emigre, Professor Rudolf Peierls, to work on the Tube Alloys Project (at £5 a week – less pay than many factory workers).

As with Allan Nunn May, MI5 failed to thoroughly check Fuchs' political background when he applied for involvement in top secret work. In 1934, the Nazi consul in Bristol had reported Fuchs as a communist spy to the Chief Constable of Avon and Somerset. At the time this was almost certainly a malicious untruth. But when this report was later handed on to the security services, it caused them a certain amount of consternation. In the end, they decided to pass him for the Tube Alloys Project, provided his fellow researchers didn't 'let him see more than was necessary'. Such an imprecise set of guidelines was unhelpful, particularly since Fuchs brilliance made his colleagues feel that he deserved to know everything that went on.

In the Autumn of 1941, motivated by Germany's attack on Russia and the realisation of what the Tube Alloys Project would mean to the world if it succeeded, Fuchs approached the Soviet embassy and offered his services as a spy. (He horrified their security people by doing this quite literally; walking up the front steps in broad daylight, regardless of observation.) A contact man was assigned to Fuchs and they met to collect atomic information every three months. This went on without a hitch until the end of 1943, when Fuchs crossed the Atlantic to work on the Manhattan Project.

In New York, he was assigned a new contact – Swiss-born chemist, Harry Gold. The meetings continued as they had in London until July, 1944, when Fuchs disappeared without warning. In fact, he had been transferred to Los Alamos, in New Mexico, to help in the completion of the bomb project. Fuchs did not attempt to re-contact the Soviets until he returned to New York to visit his sister for New Year. The reason he gave Gold for his silence was that the Americans had impressed upon him how vital it was to their national security that nobody knew where the base was. He wanted to help the Soviets, he explained simply, but not if it would endanger the USA.

Nevertheless, Fuchs was happy to discuss the new lines of atom research being pursued at Los Alamos, and passed on to Gold everything he knew. He was also persuaded to agree to another meeting, this time in Santa Fe, the nearest city to the base. The date was set for 2 June, 1945, by which time, Fuchs assured Gold, the first bomb would be near completion. He himself, Fuchs added with a touch of pride, had been chosen to be among the select group of scientists present at the first test.

The meeting took place on Castillo Bridge at 4 pm on 2 June. Fuchs explained that he could only spare Gold half an hour, since he was only supposed to be out having a drink – the Los Alamos base being strictly teetotal. Nevertheless, Fuchs had come prepared and handed over a thick wad of papers containing the latest bomb research. The project, he added was close to completion – the first detonation was planned for early the following month.

With such a precious cargo, one would have thought that Harry Gold would head straight back to New York; but he had another appointment before he headed east. In neighbouring Albuquerque, Technical Corporal David Greenglass was waiting with information almost as important as that provided by Fuchs. The soldier had been working at Los Alamos as a machinist for many months, but was unaware that what he was machining was an atomic bomb. His brother-in-law, Julius Rosenberg, enlightened him at the same time he recruited him to the Soviet cause (both Rosenberg and his wife Ethel having been communist agents for years). Money and even a wife had been arranged for Greenglass, in return for collecting information on the building of the bomb, and he was now ready to report. However, the use of Gold to collect the information was something of a breach in security procedures. Each spy should have been provided with a different contact man to keep operations separate. But a Russian courier had failed to make contact, and this seemingly minor slip was to cost them dear.

When Fuchs and Gold met again, on 19 September, 1945, the war was over – the bomb had been dropped on Hiroshima, and Japan had surrendered. Fuchs told his contact that he had witnessed the wonder of an atomic explosion, and was still, after two months, dazzled and awe-struck by what he had seen, but Gold eventually managed to get him on to more practical matters and Fuchs handed over the post explosion data. As they parted the scientist added that he was likely to be sent back to England soon. Even the friendship between Britain and the US was being stretched in the post bomb era. British scientists were being banned from certain top secret departments as the Americans began to monopolise the Manhattan Project. Fuchs guessed, correctly, that soon the British would be frozen out altogether.

But it was not until June, 1946, that Fuchs was transferred to the Harwell Institute in England. There he continued as a senior executive – and Soviet agent – until the Venona transcripts revealed his identity as a traitor in late 1949. In his confession Fuchs identified Harry Gold as his American contact man. Gold was arrested and, under interrogation, named David Greenglass as his second agent. (So the contact mix-up of 2 June,

1945 finally came home to roost.) Greenglass, in turn, confessed the involvement of his sister and brother-in-law. Within days, the authorities had Julius and Ethel Rosenberg and half a dozen other agents they had recruited in custody.

Perhaps through deliberate misinformation, Dr Klaus Fuchs entered the dock in March, 1950, convinced he was facing the death sentence. His council was doubtless surprised at the look of happy relief that spread across his client's face when he warned him he might be imprisoned for up to fourteen years. Indeed, this was the sentence passed by the judge. David Greenglass, who had cooperated fully with the authorities, received a similar fifteen years. Harry Gold was given a draconian thirty years, but fared better than the Rosenburgs, who were electrocuted in 1953.

Klaus Fuchs was a model prisoner and earned the maximum remission, being released in the early sixties. He is said to have been resigned to his fate, but was deeply hurt when his British citizenship was, inevitably, revoked. He returned to East Germany, married an old girlfriend and was made deputy director of the GDR's nuclear energy research centre.

Bruno Pontecorvo

Bruno Pontecorvo was born in Pisa on 22 August 1913, one of a family of eight children. Four of them left for England before the outbreak of World War II, because of Mussolini's repression of the Jews. A fifth went to America. One other brother crossed into France in November 1939. He was a Communist and joined the French underground after the German occupation. Another sister stayed in Italy and later married an agricultural scientist, also a Communist.

Pontecorvo gained his Doctorate in Physics at Rome University in 1934, where he studied under Enrico Fermi. In 1936 he left for Paris to study in the Laboratory of Nuclear Chemistry at the Collège de France and stayed on after the outbreak of World War II. In January 1940 he married Marianne Nordblom, a Swedish girl. They fled south with their infant child after the German invasion and made their way to America, via Spain and Portugal. Early in 1943 — at the same time as Nunn May left Britain for Canada — Pontecorvo also joined the Anglo-Canadian atomic research team. He was sent first to Montreal and later to Chalk River, where he and his family remained for six years.

He was vetted three times before he was granted British nationality in 1948 — the first time before he entered Canada — and was finally promoted to a senior appointment at Harwell in 1949. At the time of the Fuchs trial in 1950, Pontecorvo volunteered the information to the Harwell security authorities that his brother Gilberto was a Communist. By then, a trace in Sweden revealed that Bruno Pontecorvo and his wife Marianne were also suspected Communists and a watch was placed on him by Harwell security. He did nothing to arouse suspicion, although author Chapman Pincher has since revealed that as soon as Pontecorvo left to join the British atomic research team in Canada in 1943, his home in the US had been searched by the FBI. They found 'documentary evidence that both he and his wife were Communists and intensely anti-American, and sent a warning report to the British embassy'. It went to the senior SIS man in Washington — KGB double agent 'Kim' Philby who promptly hid it away (it was found years later, in the files). Worse still, there was also a misunderstanding between MI5 and Canadian security over Pontecorvo: each thought the other had cleared him. 'Had (the report Philby intercepted) been forwarded to London as the FBI expected, it is likely that Pontecorvo would have been refused permission to work at Harwell when he came to Britain after the war . . . Instead a Canadian security clearance, which had never taken place, was accepted by MI5.'

Whether Pontecorvo realized that he was under surveillance at Harwell in 1950, or was warned, is not known, but he defected a few months later. On 25 July he set off by car with his wife and three children for a touring holiday on the Continent, which was scheduled to include a reunion with his parents at Chamonix in France and with his brother and sister in Italy. He finally reached Rome on 27 August, where he stayed with his married sister. On 30 August he paid in US $100 bills for five air tickets from Rome to Stockholm. Initially, all five were one-way: after an animated discussion with his wife (which the sales clerk later recalled) Pontecorvo changed his own from single to return, presumably to allay suspicion in the event of a query from London. They left Rome on 31 August and arrived in Stockholm via Munich and Copenhagen in the late evening of 1 September. Marianne Pontecorvo made no attempt to contact her parents, who lived near the airport; instead the Pontecorvos spent their one night on Swedish soil in a house owned by the Soviet embassy, according to unconfirmed reports. Next day they flew on to Helsinki, giving 'tourism' as the alleged reason for their visit. They were met at the airport there by an unidentified man and woman and left in a car with them – to surface again later in Moscow.

Like Marianne's parents in Stockholm, Bruno Pontecorvo's relatives in Italy insisted they knew nothing of his flight to Moscow. As far as is known, no evidence was found that he had spied for Russia either in Canada or at Harwell. Chapman Pincher's explanation for his sudden departure is that Pontecorvo 'was needed in connection with the crash development of the Soviet H-bomb. He was one of the few scientists in the world with knowledge of the type of nuclear reactor required to make the essential component of the H-bomb called lithium deuteride.'

Chapter Five

THE GREAT BRITISH SPY SCANDAL

The Cambridge ring — Burgess and Maclean

The cloak-and-dagger flight to Moscow by British diplomats Burgess and Maclean in the summer of 1951 — following a tip-off from another highly-placed traitor that Maclean was about to be interrogated on suspicion of treason — quickly erupted into the greatest spy scandal in the nation's history. Today it holds the dubious distinction of also being the longest-running: still the echoes rumble on, with a number of vital questions left unanswered by the authorities after more than thirty-four years — a situation which some might consider a scandal in itself, in any self-professed democratic society.

That there was a long-term Soviet conspiracy to infiltrate the British Establishment over the past half-century, with the security/intelligence network as its principal target, is no longer in doubt. With many of the original conspirators now either dead or beyond the reach of the law, the marathon spy scandal turns on a single issue: the extent to which that network was penetrated from the 1930s onward and its present state of efficiency. It was brought to a head in July 1984 when a retired senior MI5 officer, who had himself chaired an internal inquiry into KGB penetration of the service dating back to Burgess-Maclean days — and who insists that it has since failed to protect itself adequately against further treachery — risked prosecution

under the Official Secrets Act to call publicly for a full
official inquiry into the matter.

The extent of the Soviet conspiracy was underlined by
the long list of spy trials between 1946, when Allan
Nunn May — a friend of Burgess and first of the atom
spies — was jailed for ten years, and 1984, when MI5
officer Michael Bettaney was sentenced to twenty-three
years' imprisonment, also for spying for Russia. No
single spy case, however, evoked as great a storm as
the joint defection of Burgess and Maclean; while the
sense of public outrage and frustration was similarly
reflected in each of the subsequent scandals which arose
directly from it.

These included the clandestine flight of Mrs Maclean
with her three young children from Geneva in 1953 to
rejoin her husband — with Soviet connivance — behind the
Iron Curtain, while the British Secret Service, which
apparently considered it unethical to shadow her, searched
in vain for the two missing traitors. Next came the scandal
of H.A.R. ('Kim') Philby, the 'Third Man' in the Burgess-
Maclean defection, who was officially cleared of any
involvement by the Foreign Secretary of the day, Harold
Macmillan — only to defect himself eight years later, after
first being restored to the payroll of the Secret Service he
had successfully betrayed for so long. Then there was the
scandal of traitor Anthony Blunt, the so-called 'Fourth Man'
in the Burgess-Maclean saga. Art historian Blunt, a wartime
MI5 officer and Surveyor of the Queen's Pictures, was
awarded a knighthood while under interrogation on suspicion of spying for Russia — the classic case of the right hand
of the Establishment not knowing what the left was doing.
Blunt finally confessed to being a Soviet agent in 1964, in
return for a promise of immunity against prosecution, but
was not unmasked until 1979 following the publication of
Andrew Boyle's book on spies within the Establishment *The
Climate of Treason*. Blunt's guilt was then officially con-

firmed by Mrs Thatcher in the House of Commons, whereupon he was stripped of his knighthood by the Palace.

No sooner had the storm over Blunt's treachery, made all the more heinous because of his royal appointment, died down than a new and even bigger spy scandal emerged. In 1981, author and journalist Chapman Pincher revealed in his book *Their Trade is Treachery* that the man suspected of being the most damaging Soviet penetration agent of all inside MI5 was none other than its former Director General, Sir Roger Hollis. Hollis, who joined MI5 before World War II, served as head of 'Section F' — the department responsible for keeping watch on all Soviet operations in Britain — before his promotion, first to deputy Director General and finally head of the service from 1956 until his retirement in 1965.

Pincher told how, '. . . early in 1980 the Prime Minister, Margaret Thatcher, was warned about a hushed-up security scandal affecting MI5 which was infinitely more explosive than the exposure of the Russian spy, Anthony Blunt. The Home Secretary, William Whitelaw, and the Attorney-General, Sir Michael Havers, were also told that in 1974 Lord Trend, formerly Sir Burke Trend and Secretary of the Cabinet for a decade, was secretly called from retirement to conduct an unprecedented inquiry. He was asked to give an independent judgment on the appalling probability that Sir Roger Hollis, a long-serving Director General of MI5, had been a Russian spy for almost thirty years.'

Not unnaturally, Chapman Pincher's disclosures caused a sensation. Hollis, however, was not charged with any offence, far less found guilty in a court of law for on 26 March 1981 Mrs Thatcher told the Commons the inquiry had concluded that Sir Roger was not a spy. Pincher stuck to his guns and in July 1984, the Prime Minister's statement was challenged in turn by retired MI5 officer (and 'mole-catcher') Peter Wright, who had earlier chaired a secret internal committee of inquiry into Soviet penetration of the security service. He insisted in both Press and television interviews that, 'Those of us intimately concerned with the investigation believed that Hollis . . . had been a long-term Soviet penetration agent in MI5.' Although he agreed there was no legal proof of treason, he maintained that 'intelligencewise, it is 99 per cent certain he was a spy.' He also alleged that Mrs Thatcher had been given 'a lot of facts which are not correct. She was advised by the security service, who were anxious that there should not be a high-level independent inquiry into the service that might . . . drag skeletons out of the cupboard they would not want revealed.'

Mr Wright further claimed that MI5 had since failed to protect itself adequately against further penetration and cited the case of Michael Bettaney, a serving MI5 officer who was sentenced to twenty-three years' imprisonment only four months earlier as the most recent example. He said it was a situation which had been allowed to develop because there had been a cover-up of the truth both by politicians and members of the service. 'I want to go before the Security Commission, or any other suitable form of inquiry, to argue my case,' he said. 'And I am not going to give up until they have listened to me.' The spy scandal which so many British governments had hoped was dead and buried was very much alive again.

From the outset, the hurried and even amateurish joint defection of Burgess and Maclean – which was carried out under the very noses of MI5 – proved successful beyond the wildest dreams of its KGB organizers. Its prime objective, to shield the frightened and unstable Maclean from direct interrogation and thus safeguard the identity of his several Communist fellow-conspirators in British government service, was achieved overnight. Its

Guy Burgess

many propaganda bonuses thereafter stemmed largely from the ostrich-like response of the British authorities to the situation they then faced. Stubborn ministerial evasion in the face of repeated Press disclosures which clearly demonstrated the total unsuitability of either man to hold any position of trust in running the country's affairs, served only to heighten the public's suspicion of a cover-up. The failure over many years by the security service to spot even the most glaringly obvious character defect in either man – and they were legion – or to pick up so much as a whisper of their publicly expressed radical left-wing views, likewise provided much food for scandal in the climate of anger and recrimination which followed the news of their defection. And it was not only political reputations which suffered. The status of MI5 and MI6 sank to an all-time low, causing considerable, and perhaps permanent, damage to the Anglo-US 'special relationship'. The KGB themselves could not have planned it better.

When Guy Francis de Moncy Burgess, then aged forty, and his Cambridge contemporary, Donald Duart Maclean, fled from Southampton at midnight on Friday, 25 May 1951, aboard the cross-Channel steamer *Falaise*, the cold war between Soviet Russia and the West was at its height. The mere fact that both men were from the Foreign Office – that storehouse of secrets, at the time possibly the most respected of all British institutions after the monarchy – was enough in itself to send shivers down the nation's spine. Equally, the mystery of the disappearance seemed all the more sinister because – on the surface at least – there appeared to be nothing in their make-up to fit the conventional Red spy image.

Here were two young men of impeccable family background and public-school education. Maclean, who was Head of the American Department of the Foreign Office in London, and the son of a former Cabinet

Minister, was married with two children. He had vanished on his thirty-eighth birthday, at a time when his American-born wife Melinda was shortly expecting their third child (a daughter, born three weeks later). Old Etonian Guy Burgess, a single man, was a wartime (Special Operations Executive) secret serviceman and son of a Royal Navy officer. He had been appointed Second Secretary at the British embassy in Washington less than a year earlier and his Foreign Office career included a two-year spell as Assistant Personal Private Secretary to the Minister of State, Hector McNeil.

That any two members of the diplomatic service should flee the country together, for any reason, was cause enough for alarm: and there was infinitely worse to come. Their joint defection, sensational and unprecedented though it was, proved to be only the tip of the iceberg. Its true significance lay in the fact that it provided the security authorities with their first inkling of a conspiracy for treason within the ranks of the Establishment itself.

From the beginning it was apparent that the conspiracy had to involve not only Burgess and Maclean but also one other traitor at least; one so highly placed, moreover, that he had immediate access to the country's most sensitive intelligence material. That much was self-evident, from the timing and circumstances preceding the disappearance. Maclean had long been regarded by many colleagues as the 'white hope' of the British diplomatic service. What none of his admirers knew was that 'Operation Bride', a US Intelligence inquiry into the wartime leakage of top-secret political and scientific information to Moscow from Washington – where Maclean had served as First Secretary in the British embassy – had identified him as the principal suspect. This information had now been relayed to London and the fateful decision to set an early date for Maclean's interrogation was taken at a special meeting, chaired by Foreign Secretary Herbert Morrison and with only the most senior security and intelligence officers present, a matter of hours before Burgess and Maclean fled the country. Clearly, someone within – or who was party to the decisions reached by – that august band was guilty either of monumental indiscretion . . . or treachery.

Terrifying though that prospect was, there were also clear indications of even deeper penetration of the security/intelligence network. Although Burgess had been under no suspicion until the night he adopted an assumed name ('Roger Styles') and disappeared with Maclean, it was straining credulity too far to accept that he might have returned coincidentally from Washington to London less than three weeks beforehand. Equally, it was inconceivable that the findings of 'Operation Bride', reached after more than two years of secret US intelligence inquiry, would have been made known at Second Secretary level in the British embassy. Clearly someone in Washington too had been guilty of indiscretion – or deliberate betrayal.

The fact that the first announcement of the double defection – by then a fortnight-old *fait accompli* – should have come not from the Prime Minister (whose duty it was as head of all security and intelligence services) to the House, but from the Press, served only to exacerbate the inevitable public reaction of shock and outrage. This blunder was compounded by the fact that while every effort thereafter by the British Secret Service over the next four years failed to locate the missing diplomats, the man in the street had little doubt from the beginning where they would be found – in Moscow. Nor was that based on blind guesswork. Within days of the first newspaper accounts of their midnight flight, former friends revealed that both had spouted Marxist sentiments from undergraduate days. Within a year the nation learned how both had openly admitted, long before they disappeared, to being Russian spies: Burgess before the outbreak of World War II (and his acceptance into the Secret Service), Maclean in the winter of 1950. The lame excuse that none of this had been reported to the authorities did little to allay the sense of anger and frustration these disclosures aroused. Why, it was asked, had such elementary facts not emerged in the course of routine security vetting?

And if the failure to trace them was not scandalous enough, lurid details of both Burgess and Maclean's myriad character defects had likewise long since come to light. Although they had apparently escaped the notice of both security officers and Foreign Office mandarins alike over the years, these details came into the possession of inquiring reporters after the defection as easily – and plentifully – as windfall apples. They included homosexuality (then a criminal offence, thus leaving both men open to blackmail), habitual drunkenness and a bent for brawling in public both in London and abroad. Moral standards were stricter in the 1950s than in today's permissive society and eye-witness accounts of such conduct by serving British diplomats fuelled the fires of scandal every bit as much as the thought of the political damage they might have done. As a result, each new Press disclosure gravely embarrassed a whole succession of governments, ministers and ex-ministers, by showing them to be either sadly misinformed, grossly inefficient, guilty of a deliberate cover-up – or even, perhaps, all three.

Four days after Clement Attlee's Socialist government of 1951 confirmed that Burgess and Maclean were indeed missing, former Tory Foreign Secretary Anthony Eden said of Donald Maclean's alleged 'breakdown through overwork' in Cairo in 1950, 'May I be allowed to say, as Mr Maclean was serving under me at the time that in all the reports I received the work he did there was very good indeed.' Alas for Mr Eden, he had never been in office during Maclean's service in Cairo: all of it had been spent under a Socialist administration.

Following that remarkable gaffe, Lord Reading, the joint Under Secretary for Foreign Affairs, said in 1952 that, 'Mr Maclean . . . performed his official duties satisfactorily up to the date of his disappearance.' This was more than a year after the security authorities had been warned by the Americans that Maclean was a likely traitor. And both ministerial views of Maclean's conduct – on duty or off – were in sharp contrast to those of author Cyril Connolly, who told *Sunday Times* readers, also in 1952, about his behaviour both in Cairo and London. He revealed how in one drunken escapade in Cairo, before an audience of twenty people (including his wife), Maclean had seized an Egyptian guard's rifle and assaulted a fellow British diplomat, breaking the man's leg in the scuffle. Later, said Connolly, after treatment from a woman psycho-analyst for his 'breakdown' in Cairo – and promotion to Head of the American Department in the bargain – Maclean openly confessed to a friend that he was a Communist agent.

Of Burgess, Foreign Secretary Herbert Morrison told the Commons on 18 July 1951, 'Mr Burgess was appointed to the office of the Minister of State on 31 December 1946. He was transferred to the Far Eastern Department on 1 November 1948. The transfer took place in the normal course of routine and was intended to give Mr Burgess experience in a political department . . . At that time there was nothing adverse, as far as we were aware, against Mr Burgess.'

Only a month earlier the poet Wystan Auden, an old friend of Burgess, had revealed that, 'Burgess . . . was an open Communist in the late 1930s. In New York, where I spend six months of the year, we met several times. While he was at the embassy in Washington, he was still pro-

Communist. We met last in March this year. We talked about Fuchs and Nunn May, who was a close friend of Burgess.' (Physicists Klaus Fuchs and Allan Nunn May were both serving prison sentences at the time for betraying atom secrets to Russia.) 'I asked him if he had been screened and Burgess spoke of diplomatic immunity.' A week after that interview appeared in the *Daily Express*, Kenneth Younger, who was Minister of State at the Foreign Office under Herbert Morrison, informed the House that, '. . . a security check was made on Mr Burgess some time ago and it was negative in its result.'

It was small wonder that the public was left to debate who to believe and how efficient such security checks could be. For three days before Mr Morrison addressed the House, an official of a London firm of solicitors representing the owners of the New Bond Street flat rented by Burgess, told the *Sunday Dispatch*,

'Soon after Burgess moved in there were complaints from other tenants of rowdy parties, shouts, screams, and fights throughout the night in the Burgess flat. He seemed to have a considerable number of parties, and they were always all-male affairs. Whenever I saw him, he seemed to have some part of his body in bandages. I told him about the complaints and he promised to be quieter in future. For a while things were quiet, Then one of our tenants in the flat above rang us in a panic. Early one Sunday morning she had been awakened by her baby girl, who was in tears and trembling. The noise from the flat below was almost indescribable. Soon afterwards an ambulance drew up and Burgess, with his head and arm bandaged, was taken to hospital on a stretcher. Quite obviously there had been a first-class fight. I rang the hospital and was told that he had a fractured skull, a broken jaw and arm injuries and was on the danger list.'

Later an ex-ballet dancer and homosexual called Jack Hewitt, who lived with Burgess at the time, explained that,

'Guy was thrown down the stairs by a fellow diplomat,' adding 'It was not Maclean.'

That happened early in 1949. Later the same year, while on holiday in Tangier and Gibraltar, Burgess was officially reported to the Foreign Office by the security authorities for 'indiscreet talk about secret matters of which he had official knowledge'. According to the government White Paper on the defection, published in 1955, Burgess had been 'severely reprimanded' for that blatant security lapse. How or why the details had not been given to the House earlier was not explained. In the same way the security check made on Burgess, which proved 'negative in its result', was made to look even more remarkable in the light of Cyril Connolly's account of an incident involving Burgess as far back as 1937. 'Burgess and a great friend of his', wrote Connolly in *The Sunday Times*, 'would sometimes stay with a talented and beautiful novelist . . . One day Burgess's friend came to her, shaken and yet impressed. Guy had confided to him that he was not only a member but a secret agent of the Communist Party, and he had then invited him . . . to join in the work.'

To most ordinary people, officialdom's reluctance to open up this Pandora's Box of self-confessed treachery seemed every bit as scandalous as its apparent lack of knowledge of the dangerous unsuitability of either man to work for the Foreign Office. On 10 July 1952 Mr Anthony Nutting, Under Secretary at the Foreign Office, was asked by Conservative MP Colonel Alan Gomme-Duncan if 'he would recommend the appointment of a Royal Commission, or appoint a suitable fact-finding body to inquire fully into the disappearance of Burgess and Maclean and all the circumstances connected therewith.'

Mr Nutting refused, saying that, 'a full inquiry' had already been made by the security authorities, in conjunction with the Foreign Office departments concerned. 'I am satisfied,' he declared, 'that nothing further would be gained by the appointment of a Royal Commission or other fact-finding body . . .' Four months later he told the House that no action was to be taken against the (unnamed) official who had appointed Burgess and Maclean to their Foreign Office posts. 'I am not prepared to lend myself to a witch-hunt of this character,' he said. Three years later the Government – and the British people – learned from newspaper articles written by Russian defector Vladimir Petrov, formerly head of the KGB in Australia, that both men were in Russia and had been from the start. Among other things Petrov revealed that Burgess had supplied 'whole briefcases' full of secret documents to his Soviet control in London between 1945 and 1948.

In the Lords debate which followed publication of the government White Paper – some of it based on Petrov's admissions – Lord Astor, a member of *The Observer* newspaper board, said, 'It was particularly unfortunate that (Nutting) should have used the phrase "witch-hunt" of those who were trying to find the truth. Trying to uncover treason is as much a duty as to prevent burglary . . . We have got to recognize that for the first time since the reign of the first Queen Elizabeth, we have a Fifth Column in this country that has penetrated the highest ranks of the Civil Service, and apparently scientists – even the church.'

He said that after Maclean returned from Cairo to London, 'He used to go in the evening and get disgustingly drunk in a certain club. He twice engaged in drunken brawls with some Left-wing friends, in one of which they were rolling on the floor. In each case the attack was that they had betrayed their former Left-wing opinions. This was the Head of the American Department!' He also described Burgess as 'drunken, dirty, and sexually indecent. Ever since school he made no pretence about it, in his conversation or his conduct.' Everyone, it seemed, knew

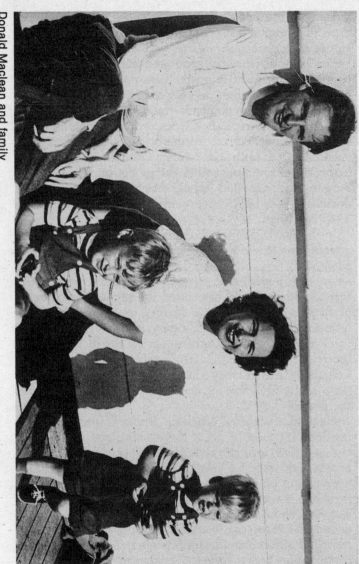

Donald Maclean and family

The Great British Spy Scandal

about the Communist beliefs and appalling conduct of these two long-term spies – except the authorities and their security advisers.

For the British security/intelligence network it was a time of utter humiliation. From the outset the Americans had been sharply critical of Britain's failure to act sooner and more firmly on the evidence uncovered by *'Operation Bride'*. MI5 had been savaged by the home Press for its failure to confront Maclean and search his home – or even maintain surveillance on him there – for fear of upsetting his pregnant wife. The failure of both intelligence and security to note and act upon the glaring character defects shown by both men for so many years was a scandal in itself. Now it was the turn of the Russians to rub salt into British wounds. In February 1956 – almost five years after the two diplomats had disappeared and with MI6 unable to offer a shred of evidence as to their whereabouts – Burgess and Maclean were produced like rabbits out of a hat to correspondents gathered in the National Hotel off Gorky Street, in the very heart of Moscow. Everything was stage managed. No questions were allowed. The pair simply issued written statements claiming that they quit England 'to work for peace', after witnessing at first hand western preparations for another war. As a propaganda coup, however, it was a brilliant success: just to see the renegade pair in the flesh again was enough to bring the scandal to the boil once more in Britain.

From then on until their deaths – both died in exile in Moscow: Burgess in 1963 and Maclean twenty years later – their value to the Russians, as both working defectors and propaganda symbols, progressively declined. With so many questions about their flight left unanswered, however, each of the several related scandals which followed their 1951 defection proved almost as damaging. The first involved Mrs Maclean and the three Maclean children.

Mrs Maclean, who did not appear at the 1956 'press conference', committed no crime when she slipped out of Geneva three years beforehand to rejoin her husband. The scandal of that wholly foreseeable development lay rather in the failure of Britain's counter-espionage departments to mount a watch on her, in intelligent anticipation of gaining the first positive clue to her traitor husband's whereabouts. It was an omission which seemed all the more scandalous when Mrs Maclean then vanished with her children, destination unknown – for Donald Maclean had already demonstrated his ability to contact her through an intermediary in Switzerland.

On 3 August 1951 – ten weeks after Maclean disappeared with Burgess – Swiss bankers' drafts worth £2,000 intended for Mrs Maclean were sent to her mother, Mrs Dunbar, then living with her in Surrey. Mrs Dunbar reported the arrival of the money to MI5 and it was subsequently paid into an account opened with the authority of the Foreign Office. News of the payment (which was proof that Maclean was in the pay of a foreign power) was withheld from the public by the authorities in Britain but discovered and published by the *Daily Express* on 2 June 1953. Since the previous summer, complaints had been made that Mrs Maclean and the children were being 'hounded' by the Press and by the Express newspaper group in particular which had proved increasingly effective. The campaign was waged largely through the correspondence columns of *The Times* under the heading 'The ethics of journalism'. Public sympathy was naturally on the side of the apparently abandoned young family, and so successful was the campaign that no one from Britain – newspaperman or secret agent – dared to follow when Mrs Maclean left London in July 1952 with her children to live first in Paris and later in Geneva. Officialdom's reaction was spelled out by Foreign Secretary Anthony Eden (the British Secret Service is directly responsible to the Foreign Secretary) after Mrs Maclean's own disappearance behind the Iron Curtain. He told the Commons, 'She was a free agent and no form of surveillance would have been ... either feasible or proper.'

It was as if the 'Great Game' was being played by the rules of cricket. Proper or not, it enabled Donald Maclean to re-establish contact with her (with help from the KGB) and the family to rejoin him within a year. On 11 September 1953 Mrs Maclean deceived her mother, now staying with her in Geneva, by pretending that she had accepted an invitation from a 'Robin Muir' – supposedly a friend from Cairo days – to visit him and his wife at their villa near Montreux, taking the children with her. 'Robin Muir' did not exist: instead Mrs Maclean drove with the children to Lausanne, where they boarded a train to Zurich and then changed on to an Austria-bound express. They were met next morning by a chauffeur-driven car at Schwarzach St Viet, near Salzburg, and taken to the Russian zone of occupation whence they flew to Moscow. Copies of the children's passport photographs, which Mrs Maclean had ordered under a false name, were later found in her Geneva flat. The date showed that her flight had been planned weeks beforehand.

Too late, two British security officers were sent to Switzerland to conduct inquiries. Two years and four months after the Burgess-Maclean defection, the KGB had notched another propaganda victory; and the great British spy scandal rumbled on.

Kim Philby

Long before Mrs Maclean vanished, the search was on within the Establishment to try to identify the 'Third Man' believed to have engineered her husband's escape. The White Paper of 1955 revealed that, 'searching inquiries involving individual interrogations were made' but admitted that, 'insufficient evidence was available to form a definite conclusion, or to warrant a prosecution.' The main target for that individual interrogation had been Harold Adrian Russell ('Kim') Philby, First Secretary at the British embassy in Washington at the time of the defection and liaison officer to the CIA and FBI.

Philby fell under immediate suspicion for two reasons: because Burgess, his friend from undergraduate days, had stayed with him throughout his posting as Second Secretary at the embassy, and more importantly because Philby – as linkman with the CIA – had been among the first to know that Maclean was suspected of treason by the US intelligence team conducting *'Operation Bride'*.

Eleven years later, a KGB officer named Anatoli Golitsin defected to the CIA from the Soviet embassy in Helsinki. Among the information he passed on was a warning that Moscow Centre, or spy headquarters, had for many years controlled a group of high-level traitors in Britain known as 'The Ring of Five'. All had been recruited, said Golitsin, during their undergraduate days in the 1930s at Cambridge University. He knew Burgess and Maclean (then in Moscow) to be two of the five and although he was unable to name the others, some of the clues he gave pointed the finger at Philby as one of them.

'Kim' Philby was a former Westminster public schoolboy and son of the distinguished Arabist, Harry St John Philby. He went to Trinity College, Cambridge, in 1929 – the same year as Burgess – and later wrote in his book *My Silent War*: 'I left university with a degree (in 1933) and with the conviction that my life must be devoted to Communism.'

If much of the book was propaganda, that was certainly true. Why the Russians selected Cambridge as their main recruiting centre was explained by Andrew Boyle in his *Climate of Treason*. 'The fact that a nucleus of perhaps a dozen Communists existed among the Fellows made Cambridge a natural choice. Although Clemens Palme Dutt nominally proposed it, there can be no doubt that the initiative came from the West European Bureau of the Committee, acting on instructions issued by Maxim Litvinov, Karl Radek and other leading policy makers in Moscow.'

Philby then spent his apprentice service as Communist agent in Austria, during the Nazi rise to power. It was there he married his first wife, a Communist named Litzi Friedman who herself became a Soviet agent. (He married three times altogether.) After his return to London, he pretended a conversion to the Right and later served as foreign correspondent for *The Times* during the Spanish civil war, with the Franco forces. On the outbreak of World War II he was sent to France as war correspondent with the British Expeditionary Force. Following the evacuation in 1940 he left Fleet Street to join the British Secret Service – sponsored by his Cambridge recruiter and fellow-spy in 'The Ring of Five', Guy Burgess. No mention of his 1934 marriage to Litzi Friedman was made until his second marriage, in 1946: even then it brought no repercussion. He won an OBE for his wartime intelligence service, yet spied for the Russians throughout, his value growing with each promotion. As head of the Iberian section he blocked reports suggesting that Admiral Canaris, chief of the Abwehr (German military intelligence), was willing to negotiate a separate peace with the Western Allies after the overthrow of Hitler – the Communist reasoning being that the longer the war lasted, the greater would be Russia's post-war influence in Europe. In 1945, Philby betrayed a would-be

Russian defector in Istanbul named Volkov, who possessed information which could have identified 'The Ring of Five' spy group, himself included. Later, as head of station in Washington, he had access to the most sensitive information. Among other acts of treachery, he gave the Russians advance warning of Anglo-US plans to parachute Albanian nationalists into that country to topple the Hoxha regime; all were intercepted and shot.

As liaison officer to the CIA, he was ideally placed to save Maclean. After first informing Moscow that Maclean's wartime treason had been uncovered by *'Operation Bride'*, he was instructed to send Burgess back to London to warn him. Burgess then arranged to have himself sent home for 'misconduct' – a series of wild driving offences: not once was he suspected of espionage – where in the natural course of events he reported to Maclean in his role as Head of the American Department. When the CIA demanded Philby's own recall from Washington a month later, all the British authorities could do – in the absence of proof against Philby – was to make him resign. Several of his colleagues continued to believe in his innocence. Much later, after he had been publicly named in an American newspaper as the 'Third Man', no British newspaper dared follow suit because of the libel laws. As a result 'Kim' Philby's name remained unknown to the public at home until 25 October 1955, when Socialist MP Colonel Marcus Lipton asked the then Prime Minister, Anthony Eden, 'Have you made up your mind to cover up at all costs the dubious "Third Man" activities of Mr Harold Philby, who was First Secretary at the Washington embassy a while ago?'

Sir Anthony made no reply; Philby declined to comment from his home in Sussex. Then in the Commons debate which followed shortly afterwards, Foreign Secretary Harold Macmillan took it upon himself to clear Philby with this statement,

'Mr Philby had been a friend of Burgess from the time when they were fellow undergraduates at Trinity College, Cambridge. Burgess had been accommodated with Philby and his family at the latter's home in Washington from August 1950 to April 1951 . . . and, of course, it will be remembered that at no time before he fled was Burgess under suspicion. It is now known that Mr Philby had Communist associates during and after his university days. In view of the circumstances, he was asked in July 1951 to resign from the Foreign Service. Since that date his case has been the subject of close investigation. No evidence has been found . . . to show that he was responsible for warning Burgess or Maclean. While in government service he carried out his duties ably and conscientiously, and I have no reason to conclude that Mr Philby has at any time betrayed the interests of his country, or to identify him with the so-called 'Third Man', if indeed there was one.'

No minister before or since, in all the long-running spy scandal, has been proved more hopelessly wrong in his judgment. In *Their Trade is Treachery* Mr Chapman Pincher, who discussed the issue with Mr Macmillan, revealed that, 'He . . . was told by the Law Officers that Philby was almost certainly guilty but was unprepared, in the interests of individual liberty, to use the privilege of Parliament even to suggest an unproven situation regarding Philby, as MI5 wanted. He was not prepared to say in Parliament what he knew he would not dare to say outside.'

As Marshal Bosquet observed of The Charge of the Light Brigade, '*C'est magnifique, mais ce n'est pas la guerre.*' At once Philby took full advantage of Macmillan's gullibility. Whitewashed by the Foreign Secretary, secure in the knowledge that MI5 had no evidence against him, and aware that such an unsolicited character reference – coming whence it did – would effectively muzzle the newspapers too, he promptly called a press conference. He used it both to lie about his past ('I have never been a Communist') and to call Colonel Lipton's bluff, by challenging him to repeat his remarks outside the House. Typically, he was to complain later that, 'Lipton had shattered my dream . . . of extracting a very large sum (in libel damages) from a Beaverbrook newspaper.'

Next, discreet lobbying of influential friends led to his re-employment as a foreign correspondent in the Middle East, based on Beirut. At the same time the Secret Service – hoodwinked yet again – used the appointment to reinstate Philby as a freelance agent in the area, under his journalistic cover. Incredible though it now sounds, he thereupon served as both British agent and Russian spy for a further seven years, until Golitsin's debriefing in 1962 reinforced all the old suspicions against him. Finally, after new evidence had come from an independent source, suspicion that he had been a traitor all along hardened into certainty. In 1963 he was questioned once more, in Beirut, when he finally confessed that he had been a Russian spy since 1934. Knowing that his MI6 investigator had no powers to order him home, Philby played for time by pretending to 'consider' an offer of immunity from prosecution if he returned voluntarily to face more detailed interrogation. Instead, he promptly defected in his turn, almost certainly via a Russian freighter which left Beirut harbour on the night of 23 January 1963. To some, it seemed poetic justice that he should have done so during Harold Macmillan's premiership. Perhaps not surprisingly, Philby's defection – like that of Burgess and Maclean twelve years earlier – was attended by an almost deafening official silence right to the end. It was five months before the Government admitted that he

Harold Philby

was indeed the original 'Third Man' — and the great spy scandal boiled up all over again.

The ubiquitous Philby even provided a whiff of scandal for the Kremlin Establishment, as well as the 'Grey Brigade' in Moscow (the Western defectors and fellow-travellers living out their dull if privileged lives in the Soviet capital), by conducting an affair with Donald Maclean's wife, Melinda. It became common gossip in diplomatic circles and was well-publicised in the West while Philby's third wife, Eleanor, who had twice joined him in Russia — at his request — left him and returned home.

Art historian Anthony Blunt, born in 1907 and a fourth member of 'The Ring of Five', was the son of a London vicar who became British embassy chaplain in Paris at the time of World War I. He won a scholarship from Marlborough College to Trinity College, Cambridge, in 1926 and stayed eleven years, latterly as a don. He was recruited to Marxism by his friend and fellow-homosexual Guy Burgess; after Burgess left, Blunt took over as Red 'talent spotter' at Cambridge. Thanks to lax security vetting later, he joined MI5 in 1940 (after first being rejected as a security risk) via the Army Intelligence Corps, whereupon he gave the Russians every scrap of classified information that came his way during the war. No great skill or courage was needed. He and Burgess shared a flat in Bentinck Street, in London's West End, and turned it into a haven of drink and plenty for their friends in Security and Intelligence, as well as for homosexuals and fellow-travellers — a veritable Tom Tiddler's ground for espionage. They then took their notes and stolen secret papers to Blunt's quarters at the Courtauld Institute, where they were photographed for delivery to the Soviet embassy in Kensington Palace Gardens. Neither came under suspicion at any time. In *Their Trade is Treachery* Chapman Pincher described Blunt as: '. . . one of the most damaging spies ever to operate in Britain, contrary to the common belief that, compared with Philby or Maclean, he was in the second division. His crimes against his country, dragged out of him during hundreds of hours of taped interrogations, are such an indictment of wartime security that every effort has been made to cover them from public knowledge.' Blackmail was carried out at Bentinck Street too. In *The Climate of Treason* Andrew Boyle revealed: 'Just to demonstrate that blackmail could be an unpleasantly two-sided affair, he [Burgess] invited his Foreign Office friend [Maclean] to a stage-managed orgy at Bentinck Street. Some choice erotic photographs of Donald lying naked and oblivious in the arms of another man were duly added, Burgess later told Maclean, to his private collection.'

After he left MI5 in 1945, Blunt remained in close touch with Burgess. On 7 May 1951 he met Burgess off the *Queen Mary* at Southampton and learned that he was under KGB orders (via Philby) to warn Maclean the net was closing round him. Blunt himself came under suspicion almost immediately after the defection, both as a friend of Burgess and because the security authorities had learned for the first time how Burgess had admitted to being a Comintern agent in 1937, naming Blunt as a fellow-conspirator. However, he bluffed his way through every interrogation until his confession in 1964. He confessed then only after new evidence against him came from American sources – and on promise of immunity from prosecution. His part in the Burgess-Maclean affair was encapsulated by Mrs Thatcher, who said that while he had no (official) access to secret information after leaving MI5 in 1945, Blunt 'used his old contact with the Russians to assist in the arrangements for the defection of Burgess and Maclean.'

Her carefully-worded reference to Blunt's role in their defection leaves open to doubt the identity of the 'Fourth

Man' in the conspiracy. In his book Andrew Boyle named
Blunt as the one who rang Burgess during the afternoon
of 25 May 1951, to pass on the precise date on which
MI5 planned to interrogate Maclean (Monday, 28 May),
thus pre-empting their flight. (Burgess had previously
arranged to leave for France on 25 May with a young,
homosexual American; their cabins on the *Falaise* were
already booked.) Others believe the final tip-off came
from Philby in Washington. Chapman Pincher put forward
another theory in his book. Blunt's denial that he warned
Burgess was confirmed by his own sources, said Pincher,
adding: 'But there seems to be no firm evidence that
Philby was told this date. He certainly did not pass it on
to the CIA or FBI, where officers complained later of
being kept in the dark. As I have indicated, there was an
alternative source nearer at hand − the Soviet penetration
agent within MI5.'

Within the framework of Mrs Thatcher's statement,
both authors could be right. The original leak had to
come either from someone who attended the conference
on 25 May at which the date to interrogate Maclean was
set, or who straightaway learned the date through
indiscretion, or − much more likely − was told in order
to take part in the interrogation. Direct contact with
Burgess or Maclean would have placed such a penetration agent at maximum risk, so that a decision may have
been taken to use the more expendable Blunt as go-
between. However, it was not Blunt's role that sparked
off the storm which broke after he had been unmasked as
a Russian spy. The scandal was not that he had got away
with it for so long, but rather that he had remained in the
Queen's service after his confession − at the request of
the security authorities. And the question which had to
be answered was − did Her Majesty know he was a spy,
or had she been deceived by MI5 in order to score off
the KGB?

Mrs Thatcher's statement to the Commons in November 1979 answered that question only in part. She said,

'It was considered important to gain [Blunt's] co-operation in the continuing investigations by the security authorities, following the defections of Burgess, Maclean and Philby, into Soviet penetration of the security and intelligence services and other public services during and after the war. Accordingly the Attorney-General authorized the offer of immunity to Blunt if he confessed ... The Queen's Private Secretary was informed both of Blunt's confession and of the immunity from prosecution, on the basis of which it had been made. Blunt was not required to resign his appointment in the Royal Household, which was unpaid. It carried with it no access to classified information and no risk to security and the security authorities thought it desirable not to put at risk his cooperation.'

It was not until 1981 that Chapman Pincher revealed that Sir Michael Adeane, the Queen's Private Secretary '. . . asked what action the authorities would like the Queen to take regarding Blunt's Royal appointment if Blunt agreed to confess. He was told that it would be advisable for the Queen to take no action whatsoever because, otherwise, traitors to whom Blunt might point could take evasive action . . . Normally writers do not really know what the Queen does or says but, because of a fluke circumstance, I *know* the Queen was properly alerted to the Blunt situation by Adeane as soon as he had received the brief of the confession. She merely asked what the official advice was, and on being told agreed to accept it in the national interest.'

Remarkably, that decision in 1964 to grant immunity to Blunt – taken by Attorney-General Sir John Hobson (a Minister, although not a member of the Cabinet) – was withheld from his Prime Minister, Sir Alec Douglas-Home. When the facts were finally made known by Mrs Thatcher – fifteen years later – Lord Home's insistence that he had never been told, completely borne out by the record, served only to add to the smell of a cover-up which had attended this long, sorry, spy scandal from the start. And scandal it most certainly was, all over again. It was one thing for the nation to learn that the Queen had become involved, in the interests of the national security – that was something all could understand, if not approve – but what added insult to injury was the realization that honours galore had been conferred on the traitor Blunt since he was first interrogated on suspicion of being a spy back in 1951.

Although the authorities had failed to unearth corroborant evidence against him, as they had similarly failed in the case of Philby, Blunt had remained a firm suspect since he was first reported to them. Indeed, he had been subjected to no less than eleven interrogations before he finally confessed in 1964. Yet not only had he retained his Palace appointment, he had also received a knighthood along the way and he continued to have further honours bestowed upon him after he confessed to being a spy. To the man in the street it was an 'Alice in Wonderland' situation. Already appointed Surveyor of the King's Pictures after leaving MI5 at the end of the war, Blunt later became Surveyor of the Queen's Pictures in 1952, a year after his interrogation had begun; he was also made a Knight Commander of the Royal Victorian Order in 1956 – an honour which led in turn to the prestigious appointment as Slade Professor of Fine Art, at both Oxford and Cambridge Universities, to honorary degrees from the universities of Bristol, Durham, Oxford and Paris, and an honorary Fellowship of his old college, Trinity. In 1972, the year he survived an operation for cancer – eight years after he had confessed to being a Soviet spy – he was appointed Adviser of the Queen's Pictures and Drawings, a position he held until his retirement in 1978. He remained Director of the Courtauld Institute, the scene of his wartime spy photography, until 1974.

Even after he was stripped of his knighthood, following his denouncement by Mrs Thatcher in the Commons, he continued to be treated in some quarters with respect bordering almost on obsequiousness. The 'press conference' to which he assented five days later was stage managed and restricted to journalists from *The Times* and *The Guardian*. Two television crews were allotted ten minutes apiece for questions before Blunt disappeared into the *Times'* board room for a lunch of trout and white wine. Its one enduring achievement was to perpetuate the belief that he still had much to hide.

The *Daily Express*, which first broke the spy-scandal story twenty-eight years earlier, growled that: 'Professor Blunt would not have been offered so much as a stale kipper in the *Express* offices ... In the event (the "conference") failed to produce a single satisfactory answer to the questions that matter.' Former Prime Minister James Callaghan observed: 'I am bound to say that I think ... there has been a tendency to treat Mr Blunt with kid gloves. That is not my view with hindsight; I expressed it as Prime Minister, and was minuted to that effect.'

What the security authorities gained from their featherbed treatment of this long-term traitor is open to doubt. Chapman Pincher's verdict was that: 'It was concluded that during his interrogations he had lied and misled MI5

RAF Caerwent, a NATO base in Kent, is one of Britain's most top secret locations. Or rather, it was until 1976, when the Forestry Commission published a ramblers' map that showed the base's entire layout in detail; including the highly sensitive arms depot.

The Commission had based the map on a series of aerial photographs and had no idea the buildings were top secret. Ever vigilant, the Ministry of Defence discovered the breach of security and banned the map – in 1981 – by which time, over 2,000 copies had been sold to enthusiastic ramblers across the country. It is not known if any of these worked for the KGB.

over some of his dealings with the Russians. It was suspected that he had met with his Russian friends on more occasions after the war than he had admitted. Further, he had not changed ideologically and was proud of what he had done.'

True to form, the cynical Blunt continued to profit from his immunity guarantee until his death in 1983. Even though he had been publicly disgraced, he still preferred the life of a wealthy recluse in the West rather than join Philby & Co. in proletarian Moscow.

More Moles

In addition to Nunn May, Fuchs, Pontecorvo, Burgess, Maclean, Philby and Blunt, the long list of traitors in British service who either defected, confessed their guilt but were granted immunity, or were caught and brought to trial between 1946 and 1984 included George Blake, John Cairncross, William Vassall, Frank Bossard, William Martin Marshall, Harry Houghton, Ethel Gee, Geoffrey Prime and Michael Bettaney among others. George Blake (né Behar, of Dutch-Jewish parentage), another SIS officer, fought in the Dutch Resistance early in World War II and escaped to England, where he volunteered for the Royal Navy. He first served as interpreter at SHAEF (Supreme Allied Headquarters) and later with naval intelligence in Hamburg. In 1947 he attended a Russian languages course at Cambridge University and joined the Secret Service the following year. His first foreign service appointment, as vice-consul in Seoul, ended with his capture by northern forces during the Korean war: it is not known whether he was recruited in prison camp or at Cambridge. During his subsequent service in London, Berlin and Beirut, Blake betrayed such damaging information to the Russians that he was sentenced to an unprecedented 42-years' imprisonment at his trial in 1961. He first came under suspicion from information given by a Polish intelligence agent who defected to the CIA. All the evidence at his Old Bailey trial was heard *in camera* but press reports claimed that he received a year in jail for each Western agent he had sent to his death.

Chapman Pincher said in *Their Trade is Treachery* that: 'Much of the effort made by Macmillan and his government to blanket the horrific details of Blake's treachery was to conceal from the British public the inefficiency which had allowed such a spy to operate for so long inside the Secret Service. The main objective, however, was to conceal the facts from the US Congress, after the Fuchs and Maclean cases had already done so much damage to the reputation of Britain as a safe ally with whom to share secrets.' It was also one more chapter in the continuing great spy scandal. Another was added six years later when, with the help of ex-prisoner Seamus Bourke, Blake escaped from his cell in Wormwood Scrubs and made his way safely to Moscow. He now leads a privileged life there, like Philby, courtesy of the KGB.

John Cairncross, one-time diplomat, wartime Secret Serviceman, Treasury official and long-term Russian spy, was finally betrayed by papers abandoned in 1951 by his erstwhile friend and Cambridge contemporary, Guy Burgess. Like so many others who were netted during the Soviet trawl of the 1930s to enlist potential long-term spies, Cairncross was recruited as an undergraduate at Cambridge. His recruiter was a fellow undergraduate named James Klugman, a schoolfriend of Donald Maclean and now also a close associate of Burgess, Blunt and Philby. Klugman later introduced Cairncross to the first Soviet agent in London who controlled 'The Ring of Five'; on his instructions Cairncross officially quit the Communist Party, successfully sought entry into the diplomatic service, and subsequently transferred to the Treasury. In 1942, he joined the Secret Service code and cypher school at Bletchley Park (forerunner of today's GCHQ), returning to the Treasury after World War II.

He spied for the Russians throughout but did not come under suspicion until after the Burgess-Maclean defection in 1951 when MI5 searched Burgess's New Bond Street flat. They found what were in effect pen portraits of a number of Whitehall officials, listing their political views, their personal circumstances and peccadilloes — all of it invaluable material for a potential spy-master — which were traced back to Cairncross. When confronted, he admitted authorship but flatly denied being a spy himself or knowing that Burgess was one. In the absence of corroborant evidence he was allowed to resign his post, whereupon he moved to Rome and worked for the UN. During later interrogation by MI5, he admitted to being a Soviet agent all along; he was not granted immunity, however, and remained abroad.

William Vassall

William Vassall spent three years as an RAF photographer in World War II before he was demobilized in 1946 and returned to his former job as Admiralty clerk. In 1953 he was posted to the British embassy in Moscow, as Writer on the naval attaché's staff. There the KGB discovered something the British authorities seemed to have missed, that Vassall was a practising homosexual; whereupon they first compromised and then blackmailed him into passing over secret documents. At no time did he come under suspicion of espionage. On his return to London in 1956 Vassall served successively in the Naval Intelligence Division at the Admiralty, the office of the Civil Lord of the Admiralty, and secretariat of the Naval Staff before his arrest in 1962. In that time, although lowly in rank, he had access to a wealth of top secret defence material which he photographed and passed on to his Soviet control. The cash he received for his treachery enabled him to live in an exclusive Dolphin Square flat, although his official pay was only £15 a week: still he came under no suspicion.

Ronald Seth said in his *Encyclopaedia of Espionage* that: 'British security was extremely lax throughout the whole of the time that Vassall worked for the Admiralty. It apparently had not known that he was a homosexual when they had passed him: now they did not discover the comparative opulence in which he lived. Some of his colleagues knew about the apartment and the kind of genteel grace with which he conducted his life, but knowing his background [he was a clergyman's son] his hints that he had received one or two small legacies from dear old ladies they regarded . . . as a satisfactory explanation.'

He was caught in the autumn of 1962, following recommendations by the Radcliffe Committee to improve security in the wake of the George Blake case. Once the proper attention was paid to his life-style, Vassall was placed under surveillance. A search of his flat revealed numerous Admiralty documents together with his spy-camera equipment; caught red-handed, he made a full confession. At his Old Bailey trial Vassall was sentenced to eighteen years' imprisonment.

Press reports arising from the Vassall case led to an official Tribunal of Inquiry, through which two respected Fleet Street journalists were themselves imprisoned for refusing to name their sources. Whatever that harsh punishment may have done to smooth ruffled Establishment feathers, it did nothing to repair the damage done, or to lessen the public alarm caused by, the long-laid Soviet conspiracy.

On the instructions of his Soviet controller in London Vassall lay doggo throughout 1961, the year of yet another espionage drama which ended in the 'Portland Spy Ring' trial. All five spies involved — ringleader Konon Trofimovich Molody (alias 'Gordon Lonsdale', and a professional KGB operative), Morris and Lorna Cohen (alias 'Peter and Helen Kroger', two Soviet agents sought by the FBI for their involvement in the Rosenberg atom spy conspiracy eight years earlier), and two more British traitors, Harry Houghton and Ethel Gee — received long prison sentences. Houghton, a former master-at-arms in the Royal Navy and now an Admiralty clerk employed at the top-secret Underwater Weapons Base at Portland, Dorset, had (like Vassall) also served earlier as a Writer and spy in a British embassy behind the Iron Curtain; in his case in Warsaw. Houghton, a heavy drinker with domestic problems, was sent back to England when the authorities became aware of his circumstances but he was not suspected of treason. Instead, he was posted to the hush-hush Underwater Weapons Establishment at Portland. There he separated from his wife (they were later divorced) and with the help of his mistress Ethel Gee — a filing clerk at the base — Houghton carried on spying by selling the Navy's nuclear-submarine secrets to the KGB. The papers were smuggled out to Lonsdale, who passed them on to the Krogers for microdot radio transmission to Moscow — from the loft of their rented suburban home in Cranley Drive, Ruislip, Middlesex.

Houghton was positively identified as a traitor from statements made by the same Polish defector who betrayed George Blake. He was kept under surveillance over a long period by MI5 and Special Branch officers, when the trail led to the arrest and imprisonment of all five members of the spy ring. Houghton and Gee were sentenced to fifteen years apiece. Lonsdale received twenty-five years, the Krogers twenty years each. But these sentences proved to be academic; all three were later exchanged in East-West spy swaps.

Frank Clifton Bossard, who was born at Driffield, Yorkshire, in 1912 was a radio enthusiast who built his first receiver at the age of sixteen. He served two short prison sentences in the 1930s, one for a cheque offence, the other for non-payment of a hotel bill in Austria; joined the RAF in 1940, and rose to Flight-Lieutenant in a radar unit by the time he was demobilized in 1946. He then joined the Ministry of Civil Aviation and by 1951 was serving as an intelligence officer in Germany. In 1956 he was transferred to Ministry of Defence intelligence, with the rank of attaché at the British embassy in Bonn. He drank heavily and ran short of money to become an easy KGB target and was eventually recruited in London. From 1961 to 1965 he handed over guided-missile secrets to the Russians for cash payments totalling £15,000, then a very considerable sum, and was sentenced in May 1965 to twenty-one years' imprisonment.

William Martin Marshall, a former Royal Corps of Signals private soldier and small-time spy, was recruited by the KGB while serving as radio operator at the British embassy in Moscow in 1951. He was arrested in a London park on his return to Britain the following year, as he kept a rendezvous with Second Secretary Pavel Kuznetsov from the Soviet embassy. Kuznetsov claimed diplomatic immunity, Marshall was sentenced to five years' imprisonment. Much was made of his arrest, which occurred at the height of the Burgess-Maclean spy scandal. Thirty years later, Chapman Pincher revealed, that far from being a counter-espionage triumph, it had been 'an absolute fluke'. Marshall was followed home and placed under surveillance, said Pincher, only because an off-duty MI5 officer stepping down from a bus in London happened to see him in conversation with someone he recognized as a KGB agent.

Geoffrey Prime

Certainly Britain's counter-espionage units played no part in the unmasking in 1982 of Geoffrey Prime, the GCHQ linguist described by the Lord Chief Justice, Lord Lane, as a 'ruthless and rationally motivated spy', whose fourteen years of undetected treachery caused immense harm to Britain and the Western alliance.

Prime was arrested in April 1982 not for spying, but for indecently assaulting young girls. When he arrived home and told his wife what had happened, he further confessed to being a Soviet agent. Not surprisingly, her reaction was one of 'total shock'. Three weeks later, however, when her husband was in custody on the sex charges, she found a plastic bag under the bed containing the mini-camera he used to photograph secret documents, pads specially designed to carry coded messages, a powerful radio receiver and a tape recorder to help him decipher coded transmissions. Mrs Prime, who was commended by Lord Lane as 'a woman of great character, sympathy and humanity', consulted her solicitor, family doctor and parents before taking the ultimate step of reporting her find – and her husband's 'confession' – to the police. Only then were the counter-espionage departments called in.

Prime's counsel claimed that the GCHQ traitor had been turned into a 'sexual and social misfit' by an unhappy childhood. He made his first approach to the Russians while serving with the RAF in Berlin in 1968, by leaving a message at one of the East-West checkpoints. The KGB response arrived via a metal cylinder magnetically attached to his car. First his controllers taught him how to use microdots, one-time pads and other standard spy apparatus. On their instructions he then applied, successfully, for entry to GCHQ, the government secret communications centre at Cheltenham, in Gloucestershire. So valuable was he to the Russians in this Aladdin's Cave of secrets that in 1976 his controllers promised him that if ever he defected, he would be rewarded by the rank of colonel with an equivalent pension. They paid him more than £7,000 and he travelled to Berlin, Vienna and even on a Danube pleasure-cruiser to contact his spy-masters. In his final year alone at Cheltenham, he took fifteen rolls of film (five hundred photographs) of classified information. Yet the two 'positive vetting' security checks carried out during his service proved negative and not once had he come under suspicion.

Prime himself decided to quit his GCHQ job and the double life that went with it in 1977 – a year after his marriage and 'playing the part of a loving father' to his wife's three sons. He became a taxi driver, but the Russians refused to let him go without first obtaining their pound of flesh. He still possessed secrets they coveted, so at their behest he flew to Vienna to hand over photostat copies of GCHQ files and to Berlin for direct interrogation. Meanwhile, back in Cheltenham he led another kind of double life, indecently assaulting little girls and drawing up a card-index of more than 2,000 potential young victims. After sentencing Prime to thirty-five years' imprisonment for spying, plus a concurrent three years for indecent assault, the Lord Chief Justice told him, 'You have done incalculable harm to the interests and security of this country, and the interests and security of our friends and allies.' And once again the Press expressed public concern both for the national security and the effect of Prime's treachery on the 'Special Relationship'.

Michael Bettaney

Ironically, MI5 officer Michael Bettaney – one of the men responsible for keeping watch on KGB activity in Britain, but who secretly aspired to become a Soviet agent himself – made his first attempt to contact the Russians only a year after Prime had been jailed.

At midnight on 3 April 1983, he personally delivered a letter to the Holland Park home of Soviet-embassy official and KGB suspect Arkady Vasilyevich Gouk, offering his services as double-agent. Already he had squirrelled away a hoard of secret documents and canisters of film at his own home in Coulsdon, Surrey, in anticipation of his acceptance. It proved to be the first of three unsuccessful attempts by Bettaney to betray his country before he was arrested.

Twice he personally delivered letters to Gouk's home, each containing a 'sweetener' of intelligence information to establish his bona fides and suggestions for different sites to be used as 'dead letter-box' contacts. Fearing a trap, the Russians made no response. Finally Bettaney rang Gouk's ex-directory telephone number direct, at a given time; this, too, was left unanswered. How Bettaney was caught has not been revealed but he was arrested by Special Branch officers on 16 September 1983 — the day he planned to fly to Vienna to make personal contact with known KGB officers there. When his house in Victoria Road, Coulsdon, was searched later it was found to contain handwritten notes of secret information hidden in the bottom of a box of glasses; typewritten notes stuffed inside the cushion of a sitting-room sofa; canisters of film in the laundry cupboard, index cards in the dining-room, a list of KGB agents in Vienna inside the electric-shaver box, and photographic equipment together with a developing tank inside a suitcase in the cellar.

Bettaney, a working-class boy from Stoke-on-Trent who once planned to become a priest, won a scholarship to Oxford in 1969. After graduating in 1972 he took a teaching job in Germany and was accepted into MI5 three years later. At his trial in April 1984 the Lord Chief Justice, Lord Lane, described him as 'puerile' but 'self-opinionated and dangerous' and sentenced him to twenty-three years' imprisonment. 'It was after careful consideration you made treachery your chosen course of action,' he said. 'It was small thanks to you that the Russians rebuffed your advances.'

Press criticism was directed more at the security authorities. Under the heading Senior Heads Of MI5 Must Roll, *The Daily Telegraph* Old Bailey correspondent, Mr Ian Henry, declared: 'An alarming scandal of apparent complacency at the heart of the West's counter-espionage network allowed Michael Bettaney to try to become a traitor. Astounding errors of judgment by Bettaney's security service superiors . . . have infuriated Mrs Thatcher, who has demanded an urgent Security Commission investigation into the case. Intelligence sources are speculating that senior heads must roll within MI5. Others are insisting that a complete overhaul is needed.'

Mr Henry pointed out that – as in the case of Guy Burgess, thirty-three years earlier – clear signs of Bettaney's impending treachery were evident before his arrest, yet his superiors turned a blind eye to them. On 12 October 1982 Bettaney appeared at Marlborough Street magistrates court charged with drunkenness and was fined £12. Ian Henry said, 'He had apparently been arrested in a babbling state, boasting "I am a spy, I am a spy."' Within days the secret serviceman, known for his pompous, bordering on arrogant, nature was back in court for failing to pay his rail fare. Embarrassed MI5 chiefs successfully managed to have the criminal convictions suppressed during the public session of Bettaney's trial.

'Bettaney, who confesses that by that time he had decided to turn traitor, was so obviously at a crisis crossroads in his personal and political life, but the signs were ignored . . . The story has striking parallels to that of MI6 traitor Guy Burgess, who also boasted of his treachery during bouts of drunkenness. In Bettaney's case it was two months later, December 1982, that he was promoted to an MI5 post . . . in control of the ultra-sensitive Russian desk.'

Bettaney himself claimed a conversion to Communism in 1982. According to Ian Henry, 'Other Intelligence sceptics suspect his violent switch of allegiance dates back further, to his (MI5) days in Ulster and later, in Dublin. The Bettaney scandal is already being seen in Intelligence circles as the most powerful argument yet for the introduction into the Security Services of the polygraph lie detector tests, already on trial at GCHQ in Cheltenham.'

The Attorney-General, Sir Michael Havers, said at the trial that Bettaney's motive was ideological. The 34-year-old would-be traitor said nothing in his own defence.

Peter Wright, author of *Spycatcher*

Instead he issued a defiant statement, which was read out later by his solicitor. It consisted of an attack on 'The Establishment', accusing the Thatcher government of 'slavish adherence to the aggressive and maverick policy of the Reagan administration', as well as oppression of the poor, workless, sick and old, and concluded: 'As my last political act I call on comrades everywhere to renew their determination and redouble their efforts in pursuit of a victory which is historically inevitable.'

It sounded like a ghostly echo from the 1930s when the original 'Ring of Five' was recruited. On 9 May 1985, Prime Minister Thatcher told the Commons of 'serious errors of judgment' by MI5 in the Bettaney case, and announced a number of procedural changes which included stricter 'positive vetting' of all future recruits.

Her statement followed an inquiry by the Security Commission, which found that 'insufficient importance' had been placed on Bettaney's known character defects by his superior officers in the Security Service. They included heavy drinking, convictions for petty offences such as drunkenness and travelling on trains without first paying a fare, and of making wild utterances at parties ('I'm working for the wrong side', 'Come and see me in my dacha when I retire', and 'I'm sure the East Germans would look after me better'). To some observers it must have sounded like a re-run of events in 1951, when similar revealing statements by Donald Maclean and Guy Burgess were similarly ignored by their superiors.

The Commission's 29-page report revealed that Bettaney had been judged a suitable candidate for MI5 *after* he had been turned down by the Civil Service Selection Board because of doubts about his 'intellectual abilities'. Those doubts, said the Commissioners pointedly, 'were not regarded as sufficient to warrant rejecting him as a potential intelligence officer . . .' Instead Bettaney was positively vetted and accepted by MI5 in 1975, although he then had one conviction (as an undergraduate, for travelling on British Rail without paying his fare). Even after his subsequent work in MI5's counter-terrorism section was regarded as 'only a qualified success', in 1982 he was transferred to the section studying the KGB's 'order of battle' in Britain — and this despite his drink problem, which then included a recent conviction for drunkenness. (He was found sitting on the pavement in the West End of London, too drunk to stand, and was fined £10 by Marlborough Street magistrates. His offer to resign from MI5 was not accepted. One week later he was caught travelling on a train without a ticket, and fined £40 plus costs.) It was while he served with this ultra-sensitive security section that Bettaney started to memorize and photograph top secret material with which he attempted to persuade the Russians to enlist him as a 'mole'.

Ironically, this disclosure of the Commission's findings came almost a year after Mr Peter Wright, a former senior MI5 officer now retired and living in Australia (*see earlier copy*) told the *Observer* newspaper that he was prepared to break the Official Secrets Act if need be to try to bring about a full inquiry into the failings of the Security Service. In its report on Bettaney, the Security Commission stated, 'We feel bound to record our impression that the ethos of the Security Service in the past has tended to be insufficiently alert to the potential security risks of excessive drinking among members of the service.' The commissioners felt that Bettaney should have been suspended following his conviction for drunkenness in 1982, and queried the decision to transfer him instead to the counter-espionage section.

Of his positive vetting test in 1981 they commented, 'We believe that this review was both superficial and inadequate, not least because of the failure to consult those who had supervised Bettaney during the previous five years. The Security Service . . . justify their decision not to call for special reports on the grounds that their review process is effectively coordinated. We disagree.' While they found that Bettaney's drink problem in itself played no part in causing his treachery, they observed, 'We do consider that the extent of his drinking, and the occasions of extreme drunkenness which became known to his superiors, provided the most significant pointer to his instability of character, to which insufficient importance was attached.'

In her report to the Commons Mrs Thatcher agreed that such an inquiry into Bettaney's lifestyle '. . . would probably have led to a cessation of his employment in the Security Service', but still insisted: 'It remains the case, however, that Bettaney's attempts to get himself recruited as an agent of the Russian intelligence service were not successful. The Security Service's investigation which led to Bettaney's eventual conviction was effective and conclusive. Although in the course of his attempts to get himself recruited Bettaney did communicate some secret information to the Russians, he was arrested before he was able to pass over the major proportion of the secret information he had collected, and the grave damage that would have ensued by such communication was averted.'

Not all MPs felt inclined to take such a generous view of MI5's belated success. Opposition Leader Neil Kinnock retorted acidly: 'No man could have tried harder to get himself recruited to the Russian secret service, and his fortunate incompetence is not sufficient reassurance . . .' SDP (Social Democrat) leader and former Foreign Secretary Dr David Owen, MP, called for a 'complaints Ombudsman' for the Intelligence and Security Services, and said it was time Britain followed the example of America's CIA and FBI by forming an all-Party Select Committee to which both services should be answerable. Mr John Browne, Tory MP for Winchester, said, 'Some of us feel that infiltrations at a very senior level, and a continued catalogue of errors, must call into question not just the management but the actual operations of the Security Service. In order for credibility to be restored nothing short of forming a new service will suffice', while Jonathan Aitken (Tory, Thanet South) asked Mrs Thatcher bluntly: 'Will you be a little more sensitive to views held in all parts of the House that some form of Privy Counsellors' Committee or Ombudsman would reassure public opinion?'

While she showed some sympathy with another suggestion, that a Complaints Committee might be appointed to deal with complaints from officers within the Security Service, the Prime Minister remained adamant, 'I do not think it would be helpful to the Security Service to have their operations and their management exposed, and cross-examination in this House would be highly damaging to it.'

Who was the 'Fifth Man'?

In the thirty-three years following Burgess' and Maclean's defection to Moscow, by 1984 only four of the five Cambridge undergraduates who became members of 'The Ring of Five' were officially named by the British authorities – Burgess, Maclean, Philby and Blunt. The identity of the 'Fifth Man' remained a mystery which haunted the government and intelligence services. Since he was almost certain to have retired – if he ever existed outside the mole hunters' imagination – the authorities were keen to let the matter fade away, but authors like Andrew Boyle and Chapman Pincher kept the scandal in the public eye.

In *The Climate of Treason* Boyle named him only as
'Basil'. He described him as an English physicist, now a
naturalized American citizen, who worked hand-in-glove
in Washington first with Donald Maclean and later with
Philby – on the orders of a high-ranking US intelligence
agent who had 'turned' him, without the knowledge of
the British Secret Service. According to Boyle, he was
'turned with ease, and on practical rather than ideological
grounds. He was not a strong character. He proved
cooperative because he knew which side his bread was
buttered on.' Thereafter he pretended to work with
Maclean for the Russians by '. . . advising him which
nuclear-programme files, and which items in those files,
should be extracted from the US Atomic Energy Commission's headquarters, where the First Secretary used his
special unauthorized pass to gain entry unattended. The
information thus obtained was carefully monitored by
the Americans before "Basil" handed it to Maclean for
transmission to the Russians.'

According to Chapman Pincher in *Their Trade is
Treachery* the 'Fifth Man' was 'a defence scientist in a
most sensitive position in the Government service. This
person is not Dr Basil Mann, the atomic scientist living
in the US and recently named as the "Fifth Man", and
against whom I am assured there is no evidence . . . The
man in question has no connection with atomic science.'
Pincher also said that, 'As long as Hollis remained head
of MI5 he refused to allow the Blunt case-officers to
interview the scientist.' After Hollis retired in 1965, the
man's telephone was tapped and he was interrogated
over a period of six weeks. He then admitted that, 'he
was still a committed Communist and had breached the
Civil Service security rules by failing to admit it on his
positive vetting form.' He further admitted to having met
the early Russian controller of 'The Ring of Five' while
he himself was at Cambridge, and other members of the

Soviet-embassy staff later, although he flatly denied that he had ever given them classified information. He further ignored an offer of immunity from prosecution if he 'cooperated', said Pincher, and 'as he was quite close to retirement – and perhaps to cover up the suspicion which could have serious consequences for the Anglo-American exchange of defence secrets – he was allowed to retire early for "personal reasons" and on full pension.'

On 22 July 1984 *The Sunday Times* printed a list of twenty-one names, which it claimed had been 'drawn up by senior MI5 officers and suspected by them of having been spies for the Soviet Union . . . The list is a top secret MI5 assessment of the suspected extent of Soviet penetration of senior Whitehall positions.' It was split into four groups, under the headings: Known Defectors; Partially Confessed; Confessed; Unresolved. Heading the list of names in Group 2 (Partially Confessed) was 'Alister Watson, scientist, dead.' The newspaper identified Watson as the scientist Chapman Pincher had described but not named in his book. The name at the top of Group 4 (Unresolved) was that of 'Sir Roger Hollis Head of MI5, dead.'

The newspaper also said that the list was 'drawn up partly by Peter Wright, a former MI5 officer who now lives in Australia. Wright represents a faction of retired MI5 officers who were closely involved in the hunt for moles within the British governing Establishment and who believe there was a cover-up to protect the guilty . . .'

In 1986, Wright published 'Spycatcher,' a rather self-aggrandising history of his hunt for the Fifth Man. In it, he specifically named the late Sir Roger Hollis – respected MI5 chief for many years – as the last mole of the Cambridge Ring. Margaret Thatcher's government tried to ban the book in both Britain and Australia, but failed in both cases. (The Australian court showed little sympathy for the open attempt at cover-up and in Britain the publishers won on appeal.) All the British authorities had managed to do was give Wright's accusations world-wide publicity.

In fact, as it later turned out, Peter Wright was totally wrong in his suspicions. In 1990, KGB defector Oleg Gordievsky named the Fifth Man as *John Cairncross* (see the 'More Moles' section of this chapter). The accusation was confirmed in 1991 by Yuri Modin, the Russian controller of all five Cambridge educated spies. Cairncross had acted in isolation from the other four and had been unaware of their existence. Following the defection of Philby, the Cambridge Ring was no more, but the mole hunters, ignorant of this fact, continued their fruitless investigations. In effect, they wasted decades hunting for a spy they had already caught. The damage to Britain's intelligence services wrought by this unnecessary extension of the spy scandal was incalculable.

Titles in the World Famous series

World Famous Cults and Fanatics

World Famous Scandals

World Famous Strange Tales and Weird Mysteries

World Famous Crimes of Passion

World Famous Unsolved Crimes

World Famous Catastrophes

World Famous Strange but True

World Famous True Ghost Stories

World Famous Gangsters

World Famous Robberies

World Famous Weird News Stories

World Famous SAS and Elite Forces

World Famous Royal Scandals

World Famous UFOs

World Famous Unsolved

World Famous War Heroes

World Famous True Love Stories

World Famous Spies